MAKE WORK GREAT

Supercharge Your Team, Reinvent the Culture, and Gain Influence—One Person at a Time

ED MUZIO

New York Chicago San Francisco Lisbon London Madrid Mexico City
Milan New Delhi San Juan Seoul Singapore Sydney Toronto

The McGraw-Hill Companies

Library of Congress Cataloging-in-Publication Data

Muzio, Edward G. (Edward Gregory), 1974–
Make work great : supercharge your team, reinvent the culture, and gain influence one person at a time / by Edward G. Muzio.
p. cm.
ISBN 978-0-07-162209-7
1. Organizational change. 2. Corporate culture. 3. Organizational behavior. 4. Interpersonal relations. I. Title.

HD58.8.M89 2010
658.4'06—dc22 2009042354

1 2 3 4 5 6 7 8 9 10 11 12 13 14 15 WFR/WFR 1 9 8 7 6 5 4 3 2 1 0

ISBN 978-0-07-162209-7
MHID 0-07-162209-8

Interior illustrations by Glyph International

This book is dedicated to my parents, Marie and Ed, who insisted on teaching their children to think for themselves under any circumstance.

It is written for Matthew, Daniel, Makenna, and Addisen, who may not read it any time soon but whose futures will hopefully be improved by what it contains.

Contents

PART 3 LEADING YOUR CRYSTAL

Acknowledgments

The most personally satisfying aspect of this project for me has also been the most beneficial: the collaboration and coaching given by my advisory board. Whatever benefit you take from this book, I feel safe in estimating that half of it would not have been there but for the nudges, suggestions, and candid guidance I received from three exceptional individuals: Bill Daniels of American Consulting and Training; Deborah Fisher, Ph.D., of Group Harmonics; and Mike Bown of Acorn Coaching. Each mentored me long before this project began; merely saying "thank you" seemed inadequate even back then! When I now consider the additional hours all three spent reading, redlining, and talking about this work, I am at a total loss for how to express my gratitude. The closest I can come is to say that the book, like my career and my life, would not be what it is today without their involvement.

I am also indebted to two early reviewers whose feedback on the final draft of the manuscript was instrumental in making the text readable and useful in real life. Offering this type of feedback is an especially thankless job because it involves bringing a fresh, unbiased perspective to an emotionally involved, potentially entrenched author. Yet Valerie Peters of Sandia National Laboratories and Glenn Hughes of KLA-Tencor were kind enough to volunteer for the job, wise enough to perceive which parts of the text needed attention, and clever enough to communicate their insights in a useful and actionable way.

I must further acknowledge the contribution of clients who have taught me, through their questions and comments, to be clear when discussing the topics contained herein. Thanks to the willingness of organizations like Intel, VeriSign, Sandia National Laboratories, COPART, Yale Law School, and many more to invest in their own development, I have had the good fortune to learn from a wide variety of professionals of incredible character and capability. Chief among them have been Steve Overcashier, Ron Sacchi, Heidi Clark, Esther Stone, Jim Foster, Robin Miles, Jim Duncan, Karen Alderman, Brian Lillie, Mitch Peterson, Erv Thomas, Donna Collins, Nicole Mather, and Shirley Maier. As you might imagine, there are many others, too numerous to name, to whom all I can offer is the inadequate phrase "you know who you are."

One individual who must be named is Marianne Wilman of CBS, producer and director of the video segments referenced in each chapter—the clips in which I endeavor to explain key topics and models in about four minutes using a dry-erase board. It is difficult to appreciate the complexity involved with this type of production unless you have experienced it firsthand. Suffice it to say that the result of her direction and coaching has been an increased lucidity on my part, one that has extended into many areas of my professional life, including this book. Moreover, were it not for Marianne, Janice Hui, Daniel Masaoka, Celso Bulgatti, and the rest of Marianne's team, the video segments referred to in the text—free tools to facilitate the electronic sharing of ideas with colleagues—would simply not exist.

Speaking of facilitating the sharing of ideas, I am tremendously grateful to the entire team at McGraw-Hill. To begin with, Mary Glenn's constant support, encouragement, and engagement have been immensely helpful. From our first conceptual conversation to the final manuscript submission, editing, and production, Mary has been a receptive and responsive go-to person for anything and everything. Ours has been an enjoyable partnership and one I hope to repeat.

Of course, she did not work alone. I offer my sincerest thanks to the rest of the McGraw-Hill group, including Gaya Vinay, Staci Shands, Tania Loghmani, Craig Bolt, Karen Steib, and the many others I did not even meet. I have only the faintest grasp of what is required to bring a publication like this to market, and I am grateful for those professionals who know so much more and implement what they know so effectively.

Finally, I must acknowledge Jeanne Wood, our office manager at Group Harmonics and someone with whom I have had a long and rewarding familial relationship as well. Her involvement in this book has been the same as her involvement in our firm: to do whatever needed doing and do it well. Perhaps more importantly, the many hours I carved out of my days for writing and editing were available to me only thanks to Jeanne's tremendous competence in overseeing other parts of our operation. If there were no Jeanne, there would be no book.

As you can see, the trusted friends and colleagues listed here hold many titles and play many roles. They do, however, have one thing in common: each works as a positive example, a recognized beneficial force, within his or her own sphere of influence. Consciously or unconsciously, each is a culture builder in his or her own right. I'm honored to be a member of their crystalline networks and to have them in mine.

Prologue

Choose to Choose

> The strongest principle of growth lies in human choice.
>
> —GEORGE ELIOT

You're not as autonomous as you think you are.

No offense. Neither am I.

That seems a terrible way to begin a book, doesn't it? Here I claim to have a method of creating your own workplace culture and making your workplace great, regardless of your surroundings. I'm promising that through your own efforts you can create a "crystal" of positive workplace culture in a sea of—well, whatever else you are experiencing right now. Take the initiative, take action, and create a great environment through your own efforts.

Why then would I possibly choose to begin by telling you to mistrust your own autonomy? Let me explain.

We Are Driven by Peers

When you're standing on an elevator waiting to reach your floor, which way do you face? Almost everyone faces the door. Why? Is it so you can watch the electronic display? Perhaps, but the behavior may well predate the existence of such displays. Most likely, you do it because that's what everyone does on an elevator.

Decades ago, in a televised series of "Candid Camera" pranks, three actors repeatedly boarded an elevator with a single unsuspecting rider. The actors didn't say or do anything out of the ordinary, except that they stood facing sideways or backward, rather than toward the doors. Consistently, when the doors opened at various floors, the rider was facing the same way as the actors.[1]

This amusing experiment has been conducted many times and in many ways. In one of the most famous, social psychologist Solomon Asch orchestrated a series of "perceptual problem-solving" sessions, meetings in which a group of strangers were asked for answers to obvious questions about the lengths of various lines. As in the "Candid Camera" scenario, all of the strangers except one were actors carrying out specific instructions—in this case, to answer unanimously and incorrectly. In the majority of cases, the subject, who was always asked last, would give an answer that matched the obviously incorrect opinion of the majority.[2]

Asch himself never concluded whether his subjects simply subverted their own opinions to the majority, or whether their perceptions were actually altered by it. But in a recent study, psychiatrist and neuroscientist Dr. Gregory Berns led the recreation of a similar scenario with a twist: the addition of functional magnetic resonance imaging (MRI) scans measuring the subject's brain activity. In the cases where subjects went along with incorrect group decisions, their brain activity suggested that it was not a conscious choice to conform but a potential change to their perception of the truth.[3]

If group pressure forces us to subvert our own opinions, that's problem enough. But it seems that it may go even further and change our actual perceptions.

We Are Driven by Authority

Would you harm an innocent person just because an authority figure told you to do so? We all would like to believe that our answer would be a firm "no." But if the behavior of strangers-turned-peers is a powerful influence on our own perceptions and actions, imagine what clear, open direction from established authority figures can do to us.

We don't need to imagine such a scenario. Social conformity experiments conducted by Stanley Milgram in the 1960s and recently repeated on prime-time news tested it directly. Milgram designed his studies to determine whether subjects would resist an authority figure whose directive was to inflict harm on an innocent victim. Subjects were led to believe, through falsified screams and groans, that they were administering electrical shocks of increasing intensity, pain levels, and danger to a fellow experimental subject in an adjacent room. About two-thirds of those subjects continued to "shock" their counterparts according to the authority figure's directive, despite pleas, screams, and even a seeming loss of consciousness from the supposedly suffering person. After pondering his troubling results for years, Milgram reached the following conclusion:

> *Ordinary people, simply doing their jobs, and without any particular hostility on their part, can become agents in a terrible destructive process. Moreover, even when the destructive effects of their work become patently clear, and they are asked to carry out actions incompatible with fundamental standards of morality, relatively few people have the resources needed to resist authority.*[4]

Perhaps most troubling about the Milgram experiments is that, when asked many years later how many of the subjects in his experiments actually went so far as to check on the health of the person in the adjacent room, Milgram didn't need to consult his notes for the answer: "Not one, not ever."[5] Even those who "successfully" chose to deviate from the *directives* of the authority figure never went so far as to deviate from the *framework* set up by that figure, despite the fact that from our outside perspective doing so would seem the natural—and moral—choice to make.

We Are Driven by Expectations

Take a moment to fantasize. What if you decided to stop working but remain employed? You would still show up at your workplace, still attend any regular meetings and still "play the part" around the office or job site by seeming engaged and productive. But you would no longer do any work. In this fantasy situation (please don't really try it!), you wouldn't tell anyone about the change. You would just wait to see what happened, as if you were conducting an experiment.

Now ask yourself, who would notice first? Most likely, you have a small core group of people who would be quick to start complaining about your newfound lack of output—or at the very least, to stop rewarding you for what you were doing before. These are the people who are most dependent on your work and most connected to your activity. They often are also the people with whom you have the most difficult relationships.

Studies have shown that this core group usually consists of around five to eight people. They are called your "role set" because they send you expectations about what you should or should not be doing (a.k.a. your role), along with the promise of rewards and/or punishment based on whether you comply. Often working in subtle ways, these people make it clear to you that if you don't toe their line, you're going to lose something you like and/or get something you don't.[6]

Now here's the interesting (and possibly scary) part: these people dictate more of your workplace activity and enjoyment than you realize. Studies suggest that a layperson can predict not only another person's role, but also his or her age and gender, using only the communication coming from the role set. If I just listen to what your role set is telling you, I can make extremely accurate guesses about what you do and even who you are—without even meeting you. For example, I could probably guess that a female project manager in her early twenties is in fact female, a project manager, and in her early twenties, just by eavesdropping on what her boss and a few coworkers say to her during a meeting. I would not need to meet her, see her, or hear her responses to guess correctly, and I would not need to be a project manager myself or be familiar with the jargon used in her job.

There's more. Not only are your workplace *actions* strongly driven by your role set, but your workplace *satisfaction* is heavily dependent upon it too. The question of whether your role set is sending you expectations that are commensurate with, or opposite from, your own internal guidance, is critical to that satisfaction. You are probably inclined to believe that, should you receive external direction that is inconsistent with your own sense of what is appropriate or correct, you will "stay true to yourself." But more often than not, such a mismatch will result not in your failure to comply with expectations but rather in your compliance with them despite mounting discomfort and internal conflict.[7]

In short, your role set can cause you to act predictably and in ways you would never choose otherwise. You may have the final vote as to what you do, but you are not the only driving force. Sometimes, you aren't even the strongest force.

We Make the Fundamental Attribution Error

What could be worse than learning that peer pressure, pressure from authority figures, and pressure from our role set all act to define and change both our perceptions and our actions? How about learning that we tend to be blind to the roles of all three?

As it turns out, despite our best intentions, we systematically discount the power of *context* to drive our actions. Even in seemingly obvious scenarios, we tend to overestimate the role of the individual and underestimate the role of the situation. This tendency was summarized well by James Surowiecki in an article in *The New Yorker*:

> *People are generally bad at accepting the importance of context . . . We fall prey to what the social psychologist Lee Ross called "the fundamental attribution error"—the tendency to ascribe success or failure to innate characteristics, even when the context is overwhelmingly important. In one classic demonstration, people shown a person shooting a basketball in a gym with poor lighting and another person shooting a basketball in a gym with excellent*

> *lighting assume that the second person hit more shots because he was a better player.*[8]

The people around you are strongly influenced by their peers, their authority figures, and their role sets. But when you observe their actions, you tend to think that they are acting from personal choice alone, and you respond accordingly.

By the same token, you are strongly driven by your peers, your authority figures, and your role set. Yet when the people around you notice your actions, they attribute them to your personal choices. You probably make the same assumption about your own actions. Remember, the forces around you act to shape not only your actions, but also your perceptions. You don't always realize the existence of the forces acting upon you, much less their influence.

After all, if you tend to blame an individual unfairly when you can see the situational factors, imagine how much more blind you are when the situational factors are hidden. The influence of peers, authority figures, and role sets is far less obvious than the influence of poor lighting! Your chances of naturally perceiving their power are quite small. You will only see them through conscious attention.

Culture Building Is a Conscious Choice

As I said earlier, you are not as autonomous as you think you are. Neither am I. It's an important fact to understand if your goal is to make your workplace great by creating a new culture at work.

You must start by making a conscious choice to drive the culture around you rather than to be driven by it. This is not a trivial matter. You're influenced by the culture of your workplace in ways you don't realize and on levels you don't comprehend. Your very perceptions of the solutions to problems you face can be more heavily influenced by the culture around you than by your own thinking!

Yet experts agree it is possible to maintain autonomous choice despite the often covert influence of peers and situational factors. Even in situations with extremely strong components of mind control, such as cult recruiting events, the conscious choice to differ from the group and stay in the driver's seat is the critical factor in reducing the interference of situational influences with personal choice. As one pair of psychologists noted, "going passively along 'on automatic' is often our worst enemy."[9]

You Are the Culture Teacher

The task sounds overwhelming. How can one person—you—possibly create or change something as big as "culture"?

To answer that question, we must be clear about what corporate culture is. Consider a definition penned by Edgar Schein, who is often credited with inventing the term:

> *The culture of a group can now be defined as: A pattern of shared basic assumptions that the group learned as it solved its problems of external adaptation and internal integration, that has worked well enough to be considered valid and therefore to be taught to new members as the correct way to perceive, think, and feel in relation to those problems.*[10]

In one sense, this is just a fancy way of saying "culture is how we do things around here." But notice that Schein's definition includes both what the culture dictates and where it came from. How we think, feel, and perceive "around here" is based on nothing but a set of assumptions about how to get things done that worked in the past and is taught in the present.

Consider these points:

- The problems faced "back then" are not necessarily the same problems you face today.
- The assumptions made in the past were not necessarily the best assumptions at the time, nor were the solutions the best solutions.
- The people who made those assumptions may not have been any more qualified to solve their problems than you are to solve yours.

- Those people did not have a crystal ball. When they created their assumptions, they had no way of knowing what you would face now. Besides, there's a good chance they never intended their assumptions to drive your behavior anyway.

Yet despite all this, the powerful majority—the crowd of peers, authority figures, and role set members around you—is constantly teaching, modeling, and exhibiting this set of assumptions to each other, to you, and to any new person who joins your ranks. And to the extent that you are a peer, an authority figure, a customer, or any other member of someone else's role set, you're teaching and modeling them too. Like it or not, through your actions, you are a teacher.

In that role lies your power to create and change the culture around you. The final decision as to what ideas you discuss and what actions you take is still in your hands, and it strongly affects your world. After all, some of the behavior of the people around you—behavior that you're inclined to ascribe incorrectly to their personal choice instead of their situation—may well have been learned by watching you!

You can choose to repeat the established precedent, or you can choose to role-model something different. In fact, choosing to differ from the group can be beneficial even if the specific choice you make is wrong. In Asch's perceptual problem-solving experiments, when one of the scripted actors gave a response inconsistent with those of the other actors, the real subject was more likely to depart from the perceived "majority" and give the correct answer. The accuracy of the subjects was highest in cases where the dissenting actor voiced an opinion that was further from the correct answer than the rest of the scripted majority.[11] Just suggest something different, no matter how far-fetched it seems to others, and the rest may take care of itself. Your departure from the norm demonstrates that precedent can indeed be changed; your demonstration inspires others to find their own voices too.

Choose to Choose

Are you now asking incredulously, "How can *my* actions influence the culture?" The only reply is, "How can they *not*?" You need only stand in the workplace and do something—anything. In the doing, you will either demonstrate more of what has always been taught, or you will demonstrate something different. Those around you—and by extension, the culture itself—will be affected. Over time, both will change.

So don't ask yourself how you *can* influence the culture, but rather how you already *are* influencing it. Are you consciously creating a miniculture around yourself according to your own design, or are you unwittingly training and retraining others to follow the negative aspects of the broader environment? In other words, are you a beneficiary of precedent or a slave to it?

The choice is up to you, and the rest of this book is about choices you can make that will make your workplace great. It's about the consistent practice of simple disciplines, habitual actions that convert you from culture follower to culture builder. It's about harnessing the power of precedent to create a positive environment around you, one of your own design. This is powerful stuff!

Before you start—before you even think about making any of those choices—just be sure that your first choice is to choose.

PART

1

IT STARTS WITH YOU

Simple, clear purpose and principles give rise to complex, intelligent behavior. Complex rules and regulations give rise to simple, stupid behavior.

—DEE HOCK

1 You . . . as the Seed

Attend any social event, visit any tavern, have a business lunch in any restaurant, and you will hear the same story. It could be called "My Problem at Work": the superior, coworker, or employee who is bringing down the whole group; the leadership initiative that has everyone tied in knots; the impossible-to-please customer who wreaks havoc with his or her disproportionate influence. Individual bad apples invariably lead to a ruined bunch—and often a ruined lunch. The final conclusion of the storyteller? "My workplace is terrible."

It's no surprise. Studies abound confirming what we already know: The turnover rate among top companies has been going up for 30 years, both stress and the absenteeism it causes are on the rise, and the members of our workforce consistently dislike their jobs and distrust the leadership skills among those in charge.[1–3] Everyone, it seems, is miserable, and everyone has his or her own reason. And every reason starts with someone else. "They" are the problems that plague all of us; "they" are the ones who make our workplaces anything but great.

The most obvious solution, of course, is to quit. This is a solution many people employ, as every company's attrition statistics attest.

Depending on the economy and unemployment rates, it may be more or less difficult to depart, but that doesn't make it harder to disengage. Studies have shown that only about 20 percent of employees are "highly engaged" and that 16 percent are actively disengaged and intentionally disruptive. The majority of the workforce sits idle between the extremes, not intentionally disruptive but not terribly engaged either.[4]

What's a manager to do? How is a leader supposed to lead? How can even the most engaged individual contributor actually contribute?

A Changing World

To answer these questions, we first must determine where these managers, leaders, and contributors are. It's no small consideration; the workplace has changed more in the past 15 to 20 years than it did in the entire century or two before that.

Workers are more connected, sending instant messages and text messages to each other at all hours of the day and night via computers and mobile devices. We are all linked.

Yet people are also more detached. A growing percentage of workers are "remote," working from home or a satellite location where they have few colleagues. Even those with colleagues in adjacent cubicles or offices communicate more frequently via e-mail than in person—although their coworkers sit just a few feet away. We are all alone.

Information flows more easily today. Internet technologies enable everything from the transfer of movies, pictures, and voice communications to asset transfer and package delivery tracking. We have everything we need at our fingertips.

Yet information is often buried and lost. Our senses are overburdened with spam, news, media chatter, and irrelevant trivia. Information overload exhausts us and disables our ability to process more. The things we need are harder to find than ever.

We control our destiny. The average person today may change careers 7 to 10 times in his or her life—and change jobs more often than that! Our future is scripted by nobody but ourselves, and we try to plan it well. We benefit from being mobile, and we think in terms of "what's next."[5]

Yet our destiny feels less certain than ever. Our grandfathers worked at one company until retirement and received a pension for their years of service. We don't even know if our present organization will exist a few years from now, much less whether or not we will be working there. Many of our job and career changes are not of our own choosing and not on our personal timeline.

From Process to Network

Before the information age, things were much more straightforward. Organizations designed and developed products or services, then produced, marketed, and sold them within fairly well-defined markets. Individuals were connected most closely with one part of the work: leaders and managers oversaw portions of the process or, at higher levels, the whole flow. But the system itself, as Figure 1.1 shows, was fairly linear. Each worker, represented here by a dot, was essentially a point in a process.

Now the information age is with us, and things have changed. Companies no longer deliver a product to a market. Instead, they manage a mix of products, technologies, and production and distribution systems across a matrix of customers, demographics, and geographical and logistical considerations. Sales, marketing, production, distribution, and product and customer support work in tandem

FIGURE 1.1 Information flow in the pre-information age workplace: the point/process model

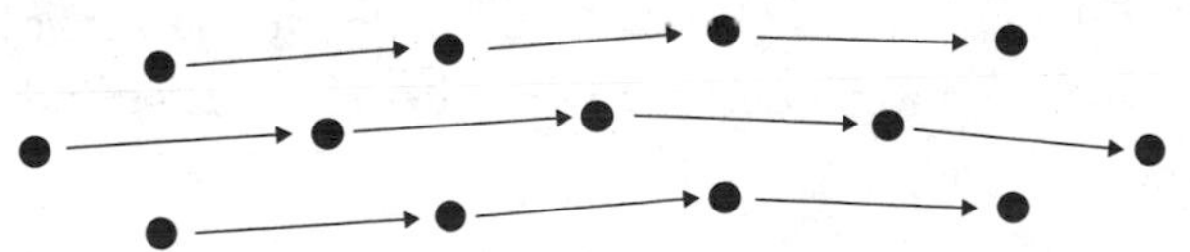

to solve a multivariate optimization problem with no clear solution. Companies that don't get it right are gone before breakfast.

Managers and employees alike share the same issue at the individual level. They no longer deliver a completed to-do list to a single superior. Rather, multiple supervisors and customers compete for their time and attention. They are given a greater workload than any one person can complete, and they often get unclear and/or highly variable direction as to what is most important. To be successful, they must interact with a variety of other people; frequently they must also mobilize staff and resources not under their direct control.

Those in management or leadership at any level face additional problems. They are the pivot points in the information economy, and they are barraged with requests for information and data from all sides. In the meantime, they must learn not only to thrive within this complex new world themselves, but to enable others to thrive within it as well.

What's happened? Whether or not we've changed, our positions have. We are now in the early information age. Thanks to the ready availability of an infinite amount of information, and the new market requirement that all of it be used intelligently in our business decisions, the picture looks a lot more like the complex structure in Figure 1.2 than the straightforward model from Figure 1.1.

Leaders expect every piece of information generated in any part of the organization to be used in other parts. Each worker has changed from a point in a process to a node in a network, sitting at the inter-

Quick Video: Burn Your Org Chart

Visit www.MakeWorkGreat.com for a short video segment about how the onset of the information age has changed the structure of the workplace. This is also an easy bit of information to share if you're trying to describe the contents of this chapter to a trusted friend or colleague.

section point of multiple lines of communication and action. Figures 1.1 and 1.2 both contain the same number of people (dots), but notice that the number of links (lines) between them in Figure 1.2 has more than tripled! The demands on each of us have multiplied. The workplace feels more chaotic because it *is* more chaotic.

How can managers support their employees in such a confusing state of affairs? How can leaders enable their organizations to succeed under such difficult and seemingly contradictory conditions? The answers lie not in the type of directives they hand out but in the type of environments they are able to create—their cultures. It's all about how they draw their Figure 1.2.

There Is No *There*; There Is No *Them*

Many of us labor under the false assumption that someone else—perhaps our employer—should provide the "right" type of environment. We naturally—and incorrectly—believe that the confusion, complexity, and apparent chaos around us must be a result of something being "wrong." Statistics abound indicating the worldwide notion that things are better elsewhere.[6–8]

FIGURE 1.2 Information flow in today's early-information-age workplace: the crystalline node/network model

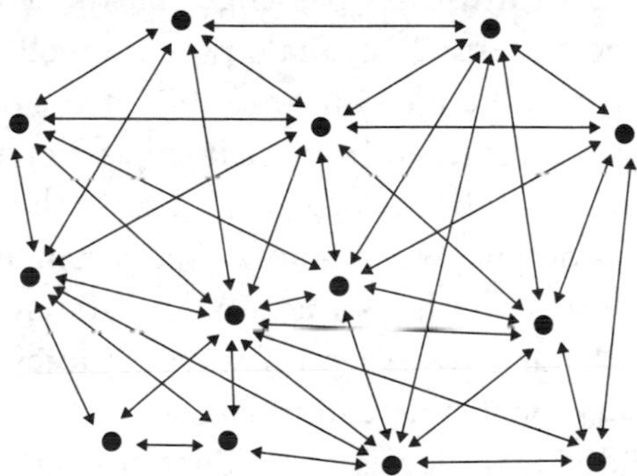

But where is "elsewhere"? The phenomenal change in the working environment isn't limited to those sitting near us; it extends across the workforce and—literally—around the globe. Nor is it employers' fault; it's just a natural outcome of the "new normal."

Recall also our working definition of *culture* from the Prologue to this book. This nebulous "environment," with all its quirks and flaws—the one that we're waiting for someone else to change—is little more than the result of accidental precedents set at a time in history when both the organization and its challenges were different and arguably much simpler. How can "it" be changed at all, if not by those of us living within it today? Many business analysts have agreed, suggesting that real change comes from within, not above.[9, 10]

Of course, some people will argue passionately that change can come only from the top. They draw a clear line between management and leadership, and they maintain that only the uppermost echelon of leaders can ever create real change. Until those leaders do something, nothing can happen. Of course, these are often the same people who go on to declare that those executives don't understand today's challenges, don't live in the real world, don't care about the plight of the workers, and so on. The "obvious" conclusion is that it is hopeless for the rest of us to try to change things.

Suggest to one of these fatalists that change can originate anywhere in the organization, and their response will be simple and graphic: asking an employee or manager to build his or her own culture at work is like asking a third-class passenger on the *Titanic* to steer the ship around the iceberg. This analogy is compelling, but it has a fatal flaw: it assumes the old, linear model of organization. Passengers below deck are detached from their ship's direction, but each employee's and manager's behavior is causal to both the company's environment and its output. We all know "one rotten apple can spoil the whole bunch"; indeed, that's the problem statement for many of our workplaces! But it works both ways. Studies confirm that any individual's emotional state can influence a whole group.[11] This extends to that individual's levels of productivity, engagement, and honesty. There are no passengers in the information age workplace.

There are also no managers who don't need to be leaders. The difference between management and leadership has been quashed by the migration from the point/process model to the node/network model of work. If *leadership* can be defined as the ability to inspire people to take action that creates change,[12] then successful management in today's workplace requires leadership at all levels—even traditionally nonmanagerial ones. In our new, chaotic, information-rich world, almost everyone must acquire information and resources from sources outside of his or her direct control. To do so requires that we get those sources to follow us voluntarily by inspiring alignment and new direction.

So it is the most influential members of the group and the most visible demonstrators of the cultural precedents who are uniquely positioned to effect change in the immediate environment in either a positive or negative way. These include leaders or managers at any level and any well-regarded individual contributor who trains, teaches, or mentors others in any capacity. Our title and organizational level don't matter as much as our reach does. The more people to whom our actions provide role-modeling, the more environmental influence we exert.

This book is about becoming—and being—one of those influential group members. It is about exerting influence on your environment by role-modeling new patterns of behavior to the people around you. It is about the regular practice of two core competencies: *being overt about tasks*, which means fully defining and transparently communicating your activity and output, and *seeking clarity within relationships*, which means being intentional and behaving evenly when interacting with others. These competencies, when practiced as disciplines, are the seeds you plant that grow a new set of workplace patterns.

The Story of Emma

I have been lucky enough to work under some truly effective leaders and culture-builders. One of the best knew all about the impact of her actions and how to consciously create an environment that encouraged people toward positive results. In this book, I will call her Emma.

Emma had been around a long time. She'd started with the company when it was very young and before it skyrocketed; her employee identification number had more leading zeros than anything else. As the company grew, so did her formal and informal influence. By the time I worked for her, she was connected—directly or indirectly—to many of the influential leaders and performers within our organization. She had direct authority over only a small number of people, but she had the respect and trust of many more high performers.

Enter a young, green Edward Muzio. It was early in my professional career, and I was excited about the opportunity to serve as a technical liaison between two manufacturing organizations. If you imagine a shop that makes ceramic tiles and a factory that uses those tiles to produce complex mosaics, you'll have a basic understanding of my position: I worked for the tile shop but was located at the mosaic factory; I was tasked with making sure that tiles were stored and handled properly after they arrived and before they were used.

It doesn't sound like much of a job, but that's because the simplified analogy misses a few things. Each of the "tiles" required millions of dollars in specialized capital equipment and tens of thousands of dollars in materials and labor to produce. These quasi-magical tiles could only be produced in one shop in the world, one at a time, and never as fast as demand warranted. The factories that used them made tens—even hundreds—of different kinds of "mosaics," and each kind required dozens of different tile types as well as multiple duplicates of each type. Not to overinflate the importance of my first position, but storage and handling was sort of a big deal.

Still, I have to admit, the job wasn't all that difficult. Not until about six months after I started, when it suddenly became technically impossible to create duplicate tiles at the level of exactness the mosaic makers needed.

It would have been nice had someone made that announcement. If someone on either side had stood up and proclaimed, "Guess what?

Tile duplication doesn't work anymore." It would have saved a lot of work. Of course, nobody did that because nobody knew: the technology had gotten ahead of us. Tiles were still being produced by the tile makers within the proper specifications and shipped as usual to unsuspecting users. The subtle differences between the duplicates were unknown to everyone and were not revealed by any standard measurements. The results only showed up as faulty mosaics—a wave of bad output with only a vaguely understood relationship to its cause, and a multimillion-dollar impact to the company's revenue stream.

Imagine the chaos.

Imagine also that young, green Edward Muzio found himself in the eye of a storm. Mosaic production experts were sure (and only grew surer) that the problem lay in the tiles; they asserted the ineptitude of the tile shop for both producing useless material and failing to realize the error. Unable to get their tiles elsewhere, they began ordering "extras" and randomly throwing away those that didn't seem to work. Tile makers maintained that everything they were producing was within factory-mandated specifications. The factory had to be doing something else wrong, and the extra orders were crippling the tile shop. Both sides yelled and screamed about the millions of dollars being wasted, the hundreds of hours being lost, and the lack of competence on the other side. And both sides vented their wrath on young, green Edward Muzio—the only person they knew to be directly connected to the other side—and said, "*You* had better make *them* fix it and *fast*!"

It's interesting what stands out in memory. I remember most clearly being worried about my career. I remember working long hours, gathering all sorts of information, and enduring abusive comments born from the frustration of technically brilliant people on both sides of the problem who had no reason to believe that the fault was theirs. I remember gathering experts, holding frequent meetings, and arranging for a seemingly endless parade of material transfer and special-handling measurement logistics. When we finally figured out that the cause was a combination of technical limitations on both sides, I remember developing information-sharing systems and writing procedures to facilitate tighter process matching between both organizations. I also remember being recognized and rewarded for my role in getting us to a practical, feasible solution.

Honestly, though, I have to think a lot harder to remember what Emma was doing during that time.

I can recall having meetings with her in which she asked lots of questions about what was going on and listened carefully to my answers. She helped me—perhaps even forced me—to be very specific about what I was trying to accomplish and what it would take to do it. Many of our conversations also centered on who in each organization was helping me and who was inadvertently getting in the way of my progress. If I reflect even more, I don't remember many of those conversations being repeated. There were a few that she couldn't influence, but most of the troublesome people became less troublesome after Emma heard about them.

I also recall that she flew out to the mosaic factory for a visit, but it wasn't just to see me. She spent a lot of time with local management and explained my progress, using words and materials I had authored. I was in the room with her, and she repeatedly credited me for the work. I remember being surprised at her demeanor. Emma has always been a soft-spoken, kindly woman who smiles a lot and makes warm eye contact when she speaks. As she sat in the room with a small handful of aggressive, hard-charging factory managers—who were responsible for millions of dollars worth of daily output—I worried that if she didn't become more aggressive, she would be bowled over by these forceful and often impatient men. She was neither. She stayed consistent in her presentation and style. She listened and learned, and yet she gave no ground on which parts of the problem were hers to manage as she saw fit. Much to my surprise, she influenced them. By the end, they were smiling and listening more than I'd seen them do before.

That's about all I remember of Emma's involvement. If, at the end of the project, you had asked young, green Edward Muzio what Emma had done, he probably would have said that she was a supportive manager and he appreciated it. You know, a polite way of saying, "Not much." After all, I did all the work, right?

Years after our professional relationship ended, we were reminiscing as friends over tea, and the situation came up. "I knew that you would get it figured out if everyone would just stay out of your way," she told me with a smile. "So I kept them out of your way." Then she told me the real story.

Working behind the scenes to reduce the impact of problematic people was the tip of the iceberg of Emma's involvement. She campaigned constantly and silently to keep me on track. Senior management at the tile shop wanted to replace me with someone more seasoned, whose experience was commensurate with the financially large and frightening nature of the problem. Emma showed them what I was doing and convinced them that I was best suited to solve it because I understood both sides. Operations management didn't want to support my investigative measurements; the shop was overloaded with orders already! Emma convinced them to do so despite their objections. Then she talked with tile-making line workers, those tasked with the actual measuring, to teach them the importance of what they were doing. Meanwhile, she leaned on people she knew in the mosaic factories, reassuring them of my competence and soliciting their support. To save me a little time, she even loaned me her administrative assistant to type up the notes from my problem-solving meetings.

Emma may have been my manager, but she was definitely a leader. She worked within her well-established network of influence to pave the way for my progress. She taught people the value of what I was doing and how to support it. She taught her fellow managers to allow the problem to be solved by not meddling and producing more chaos. She taught some fairly pushy factory executives how to listen a little better. And along the way, she taught me what I was capable of by allowing me both to do the work and to benefit from it.

I didn't remotely appreciate it at the time, but what Emma did amounted to cultural change. She created an environment in which I had a reasonable chance of success within a broader context that wouldn't have allowed it. Then she left the rest to me.

Starting a Cultural Crystal

If you have ever seen ice form or played with an elementary crystal-growing science kit, you know that crystals are formed in a predictable yet irregular pattern. They start with a small unit or seed crystal of the material that is structured in a certain way, then they grow irregularly as additional material attaches to that unit and "learns" how to organize in the same way. The creation of the initial seed, or *nucleation*, usually happens slowly and sometimes accidentally; the subsequent growth of the crystal can be much faster. One good example of this is the creation of ice on a pond when the temperature falls just below freezing; one or more areas freeze slowly and then the new pattern spreads out from there. (That's why airlines are so diligent about wing de-icing: just a few ice crystals on the wing at takeoff can easily "teach" airborne moisture to join them as wing ice during flight, an example of the type of crystal growth you definitely don't want!)

How can you most effectively make an impact on the world around you? The answer is the same whether you are a CEO, a first-line manager, a line worker, or an executive: grow a crystal. Start first with yourself, then move to the people around you, and work outward from there to improve the network around you (see Figure 1.2).

You are the seed, and you can show those around you how to organize in a new way. Affecting this type of change in your immediate environment—and by extension, building or changing the culture around you—works like the creation of a crystalline structure. You begin alone, as you envision the type of change you would like to make. Then you reach out—first to one or two people, then to a few more—and your crystal slowly grows. With it grows your reach, your influence, and the stability of the mini-environment you are attempting to create. Large crystals, after all, are far stronger than small ones. After enough cold weather, you can drive your truck out onto a frozen lake. Just don't try it too early in the winter.

Emma's cultural crystal—although she didn't call it that—was already well formed when I met her. She knew all about how to shape the environment by using her power to *demonstrate* as a power to change. Like all good culture builders, she had built her miniculture slowly over time, developing a stable base of people with whom she shared mutual trust and support. She was routinely overt about tasks and constantly sought clarity within her relationships. And it worked. Her reach was large enough to change the working environment for me, a new employee who was—physically and metaphorically—a thousand miles from the rest of her organization.

I had no idea of my good fortune in being allowed to join Emma's crystal. Being part of that miniculture allowed me to succeed when the surrounding world never would have let me. Her crystal was ready for me, and I was ready for it; that is to say, she set the precedents, and I did the work. And the impact lives on today, years later. My career success at that company snowballed, leading to many more successes and opportunities for growth. Perhaps most telling is the fact that I still count Emma as a friend, even so many years later. If she ever called to ask for anything, I wouldn't hesitate to provide it.

Of course, Emma benefited too. Her reputation and influence both grew: not only had a member of her team solved a difficult technical and organizational problem, but she had predicted it in advance. She'd told the rest of the organization that I would do it. When I did, her credibility got the same boost that mine did. As the latest addition to her cultural crystal, I added both reach and stability.

Building Your Crystal

Crystal building is like investing: it pays off if you do it consistently and patiently. Given the transitory nature of today's workplace, it may well be the most important investment you make—not only in your company's future but in your own. Your crystal may well outlive your employer! Yet it needn't be painfully serious nor exhaustively time-consuming. Crystal building is a discipline you practice a little at a time to slowly create a major shift.

Think of this book as your guide to the craft. It outlines rules and strategies, defines the parameters, and offers tactics to help you succeed. It addresses questions about how to use your precious few crystal-building minutes each day or week and issues such as how to expand your crystal, who to include, and what to do as it grows.

At its core, crystal building is simple. It requires only the disciplined practice of overtness about tasks and clarity within relationships, two competencies we will discuss in detail in the next two chapters. Through the demonstration of these patterns, you also encourage as many qualified people to attach to your crystal as you can, and you allow those people to become as successful as possible.

If you're successful (and consistency equals success), you'll influence a new set of patterns and relationships that will make you and the others in your mini-environment more productive and more satisfied with your work. Along the way, it's a good bet you'll reduce stress, enjoy your workplace more, and get more done too. Improving the network around you is good for everyone in it.

Don't Quit Your Day Job

Does "changing the immediate environment" equal "changing corporate culture"? Yes and no.

Changing corporate culture is a favorite topic among both business authors and academics. To look at an organization or a company as a system, make claims as to what changes the system needs, and then implement those changes systemwide is a compelling holy grail quest. Unfortunately, it is always an uphill battle, one with a poorly defined battle plan.[13] Perhaps even more unfortunately, for most managers and leaders, it is a different uphill battle than the one they face in delivering their required results day in and day out. Even if success is possible (and no such guarantee exists), the system-overhaul type of culture change can't get the time and attention it requires to succeed.

Creating a cultural crystal—changing your immediate environment—is not that kind of culture change. It does not involve a top-down initiative, an assessment of your company's current culture, or a battle plan for you to go out and change your workplace. No matter who you are—or who you think you are—in your organization, you likely lack the time, energy, influence, and knowledge of the intricacies of others' work to bring such a plan to fruition. You already have a job, and such a quest-as-side-project is a recipe for failure and disillusionment.

The approach we will take in this book is more moderate. You begin this minute with a seed crystal that contains you and only you. In this section we will strengthen that platform—in other words, we'll make sure that, as the nucleus of your crystal, you have created an individual version of the structure you would like to replicate. Then we'll go on to build from there. In the meantime, as you begin to think of yourself as a crystal builder, remember the following four simple guidelines that define our special type of moderation.

Don't Jeopardize Your Career

No model for successful organizational change on any scale suggests that it should be spearheaded by someone who is incompetent. Whatever else you do as a result of reading this book, keep doing your job well, and keep your workplace relationships as positive as possible. We will discuss ways of doing this in future chapters; many other resources exist that can help.* Even if you decide to abandon your current employer and seek a new position elsewhere, conduct your transition professionally and in an orderly fashion. To create a stable cultural crystal, you must *be* competent, and you must be *seen* as competent. If you interpret anything presented in this book as an invitation to do otherwise, you have misunderstood.

Don't Compromise Your Ethics

There are many good reasons to remain honest and ethical in the workplace; some of the best are addressed in works of philosophy

---

*While fully acknowledging my obvious bias, I humbly offer one: *Four Secrets to Liking Your Work* by Muzio, Fisher, and Thomas (FT Press, 2008). In this book my coauthors and I endeavored to get very specific about how to perceive the needs and tendencies of those around you and adjust accordingly to maximize both productivity and enjoyment in workplace relationships (see www.LikeWorkAgain.com for more information).

and religion that are beyond the scope of this book. When elements of your workplace encourage or even hint that you should go outside your ethical comfort zone, the decision of how to respond is always an important, deeply personal one and should never be approached lightly.

It is not the intent of this book to encourage any behavior that is even remotely unethical. You'll see as you read that quite the contrary is true: our purpose here is to encourage honesty and transparency even in the most difficult situations. Again, should you interpret anything presented here as an invitation to act outside the bounds of ethical behavior, you have misunderstood and should quickly seek a different interpretation.

Don't Use All Your Time

The intent of this book is to teach crystal building as a disciplined, regular practice that requires a small amount of time each and every workday. As a professional, you are more than capable of managing your own time, and you may choose a fixed or flexible schedule to suit you. Be advised, though, that if this activity begins to get in the way of other tasks—either competence in your job, as mentioned earlier, or your life's other priorities—you may be spending too much time at it. As with exercise or investing, the key here is a reasonable and steady habitual regimen that you can stick with over the long term, not a short burst of activity followed by burnout.

Don't Get Impatient

Sprinters and marathon runners have very different jobs. In recent years, we have come to evaluate the work of organizations as if it were a sprint, with quarterly and annual results becoming the primary measuring sticks for success. We're driven by what we define as market forces, and market forces are driven by earnings reports. So we keep our eyes focused on only a few weeks or months from today.

Culture change—and, arguably, organizational output—is a long-term endeavor. Successful companies last years and decades; they do so with well-established foundations of capability and capacity. These foundations are based on the natural processes of human interaction. They grow a little at a time, and they can only be adjusted a little at a time. No amount of additional resources like people or money can speed up the natural process—as Fredrick Brooks reminded us, nine women can't make a baby in one month.

Don't try to hurry the process by throwing too much time and energy at it. Instead, try to avoid conscious or unconscious expectations of giant changes happening in a short period. Just work on the environment around you a little each day, and stay tuned for what happens next. Small changes pave the road to progress, and they tend to have a more lasting effect than giant ones.[14]

Why Bother?

Why bother with this at all? In the most immediate and personal sense, you do this for yourself. We furnish our homes and tend to our gardens because we want to live in a comfortable environment. By the same token, we must tend to our work environment because that's where we spend about half our lives.

But know also that your results will reach far beyond your own experience. Certainly the environment you create helps those around you, but it goes further. Imagine your crystal growing larger and eventually connecting with other crystals, positive environments created by other crystal builders like yourself. How many such overlapping crystals would it take to change the definition of *normal* in your workplace? How many icy areas must intersect before you say the pond has frozen over? For a change in culture, you only need a change in precedent; for a new precedent, you merely need a number of other people who are already following it. How many is "a number"?

You could be the first nucleus, the original seed crystal. You could be a "culture of one." After all, if the current culture is an accidental amalgam of precedents based on how things used to be, why shouldn't your intentional action today ultimately transform the precedents of tomorrow? Why shouldn't you be the one who initiates a chain reaction that ultimately makes your entire workplace great? In that sense, what you're doing is full-scale cultural change.

Or perhaps not. Maybe you'll just make your own work life better and help your colleagues and employees a little as well. Maybe just a little "great" is all you need. Either way, you win. And either way, you'll still be getting your work done.

EXERCISES

1. Obtain a notebook that you can use to record your thoughts and ideas as you work through this book and your responses to the exercises at the end of each chapter. Title a blank page "Notes on Current Culture" and divide it into two columns, "Positive" and "Negative."

2. List the positive aspects of your work environment in the appropriate column. What is already great? More specifically, which traditions, precedents, and cultural elements serve you and your employer well? What existing patterns should be kept?

3. List the negative aspects of your work environment in the other column. What is not so great? More specifically, which traditions, precedents, and cultural elements are detrimental to your work experience and/or to your employer? What existing patterns should be changed?

4. Imagine inducting a loved one, who so far has been a complete outsider to your work life, into your company. Envision yourself explaining all of the politics and processes that get the work done. Which of those politics and processes make you proud? Add those to your list of positives. Which of them embarrass you? Add those to your list of negatives.

5. Start a new page and call it "Notes on Current Relationships." List about five people at work with whom you have positive, mutually supportive relationships. If possible, choose people with whom you interact on a regular basis.

---

6. On the same page, list about five people who have a lot of control over what you do at work. They may be managers, customers, employees, coworkers, or others who are most instrumental in defining your activities. Note anyone who is on both lists.

---

2 Overtness About Task

Whoever you are, whatever your position or level of authority, it all starts with you. You are the seed of the cultural crystal that you will create.

You may have gotten that idea from the book's title. You're reading *Make Work Great*; it should be apparent by now that you are the one who will do the making.

You may have drawn that conclusion from the Prologue, which closed by inviting you (and no one else) to "choose to choose"—that is, to make the conscious choice that you will be a setter of precedent, not a slave to it.

You probably got the same idea from reading the last chapter, with all its talk about you being the nucleus and demonstrating to others how to organize and attach.

Hopefully, you felt you were in the driver's seat while you did the Chapter 1 exercises. If you skipped them, please consider returning to them now. They don't take long, and they're designed to get you thinking and acting like the person at the center of it all.

That's who you are. I'm repeating this message because it seems to be one of the hardest for people to hear. Many of us were trained by example to externalize the sources of our environmental problems: an incompetent teacher, a distracted parent, a thoughtless driver, an uncaring coworker, a disengaged boss. "They" inadvertently (or intentionally) create the negative environment that "we" are stuck tolerating.

Others might be inclined toward self-blame. Saying to yourself, "If only I were ______, but I'm not," instills hopelessness and suggests unsolvable inadequacy on your part. This may seem like the opposite of blaming "them," but in reality, it's just an alternative path to the same destination—avoidance of responsibility for finding an answer.

Whatever the problem, whatever its cause, *you* are the solution. You are going to teach others, by example, to use some new patterns of activity. To do that, you need to get comfortable with them yourself.

The Critical Ratio

Working is about . . . work! An organization is simply a group of people and resources put together in a way that is designed to produce value. In most cases, a big part of the plan is to convert that value to financial profit. But even organizations that don't seek financial profits, such as governments and charitable entities, attempt to produce value of some kind. If you want to effect a change in the culture of your workplace, you must demonstrate a set of patterns that, at a minimum, produces the output your organization requires. Better yet, you should endeavor with your patterns to improve upon what has been possible in the past. Either way, output is the starting point. Arguments for morale and satisfaction only hold water when they're tied to practical results; you get a paycheck in return for the work you do, not for the happiness you engender around you.

At the same time, your output must not come at too high a human cost. We all burn midnight oil and cut corners on workplace relationships occasionally, such as when we're on a tight deadline or an emergency arises. But if your normal method of producing output involves working endless hours or stepping on those around you, in addition to some ethical concerns, you have serious problems from a culture-change perspective. First, the patterns you're demonstrating are not scalable; there are only so many hours to use and so many colleagues to trample. Second, your strategy is destined to fail eventually; life will intervene with other priorities, you'll burn out, or someone whose toes you stepped on in the past will return to even the score.

Creating value is a balancing act, perhaps the most important one you perform. You must work not just to increase your output, but to optimize your ratio of output to stress. That's the critical ratio: output divided by stress. You have to arrange your work life so that you function as well as possible, while being (and appearing) as relaxed as you can be. In doing so, you increase your level of influence on others, improve your long-term career prospects, and add to the attractiveness of the patterns you're demonstrating. In the process, you probably also improve your health.

Critical ratio: $\dfrac{\text{Output you produce}}{\text{Stress you experience or create}}$

Let's not be naive. Things will never be perfect. There will always be stress at work. That's why you need to focus your attention both on what you're doing and on how you're doing it; in other words, on both parts of the output-stress ratio. Just a little focus goes a long way. Remember, small achievable steps are what you're after.

This isn't nearly as difficult or open-ended as it might sound. To begin, you just need to be overt—that is, transparent and obvious—about six aspects of your work: purpose, impact, incentives, progress, resources, and capability.

By practicing the six specific types of overtness, you will automatically guide your attention toward improving your own output-stress ratio.

As you read about the six types of overtness in the following sections, you may start to wonder with whom you're supposed to be overt. For now, we'll make things easy: think only in terms of yourself. Consider how you can become more explicit about each item in your own mind, without worrying about anyone else. Later, we'll return to the question of sharing your newfound insights with others.

Performance and Effectiveness

William Daniels defines three key components to making an individual contributor highly effective: (1) clear goals and objectives; (2) control of necessary resources; and (3) immediate, reliable feedback.[1]

Geary Rummler and Alan Brache define six performance factors that support high performance: (1) clear performance specifications—procedures, output, and standards; (2) necessary support—resources, priority, authority, time, and encouragement; (3) clear consequences—motivation, incentives, and rewards; (4) prompt feedback—performance versus expectations and praise; (5) necessary skills and knowledge—training and learning to perform; and (6) individual capability—experience and physical, mental, and emotional capacity.[2]

Clark Wilson defines six areas of a sequence used by managers who are successful at producing output through others. Abstractly, they are (1) goals, (2) planning, (3) execution, (4) feedback, (5) adjustment, and (6) reinforcement.[3]

Ken Blanchard and Sheldon Bowles identify three elements that "turn on" the people in an organization: (1) clear and meaningful goals, (2) resources and the clarity to achieve them, and (3) encouragement and support for progress.[4]

The commonalities in these lists (and elsewhere) are the basis for the six types of overtness presented here.

1. Be Overt About Your Purpose

What are you trying to do? It's amazing how difficult it can be to answer that question in a meaningful way. If you're sitting at a computer, you might answer that you're checking your e-mail. If you're attending a staff meeting, you might say that you're trying to learn something—or perhaps just stay awake. If it's early in the day, you might read off some of the items on your to-do list.

All of those replies may be honest and accurate, but none of them really answers the question of your purpose at work. The issue of why you are there—what value you produce in return for your paycheck—is the first and most important form of overtness. We often overlook this question because we mistakenly assume that the answer is self-evident. It rarely is.

Consider Peter, a successful leader with years of public sector experience. He was elated to be appointed by his state's governor to head an agency concerned with education. The "purpose" of his new position seemed obvious: to run his agency to produce the maximum benefit to its clients. That's what his job description said, that's what the governor requested, and that's what the press release announcing his acceptance claimed. What else could his purpose possibly be?

The real answer turned out to be quite complex. Certainly, he was supposed to run his agency to support its clients. But there was also a long list of constituents—parents, community groups, and city governments, for example—to whom Peter had responsibilities. Much of his time was spent interacting directly with those groups or working on their concerns and issues. He also had to represent the governor at certain state functions and serve as chairperson for some annual conferences, mainly to sustain and improve public support for his agency. As it turned out, less than half of Peter's time was spent directing actual agency work toward client benefit.

Whether this list of responsibilities was objectively "good" or "bad" is debatable, but the important question is whether Peter understood the list. At first, he didn't. Laboring under the false assumption that he was supposed to be running the agency and serving its clients at all times, he felt frustrated and distracted by more than half of his work! And because he thought of "everything else" as an interruption, he failed to differentiate between legitimate non-client-related activities and useless distractions. As a result, he didn't give important projects the attention and resources they needed, and he didn't cancel or avoid the distractions. Failing to be overt with yourself about your purpose can be a costly mistake.

Often, like Peter, you must discover your workplace purpose through trial and error. The job description and training you were given when you arrived probably told just a fraction of the story.

In actually doing the work, you may have discovered new responsibilities upon you, new relationships that have become important, and new output that you must deliver. Recall from the Prologue the definition of your role set: the small group of people who influence your actions the most. They may or may not have had anything to do with writing your job description, but they are the ones setting your agenda and demanding your time. Determining what they expect will go a long way toward discovering your workplace purpose.

Discovery of your workplace purpose is the first step; expressing it in a form that is memorable and meaningful is the next. This can be tricky because you must conceptualize it at an appropriate level of detail. You could, for example, express your purpose as a to-do list of several hundred items. That might be accurate, but it's not easily memorable or describable. At the opposite extreme, you could express your purpose as "keeping the boss happy" or "supporting customers." Such statements are concise and memorable but not particularly meaningful; they could easily apply to many different jobs.

A summary outputs list lies between these two extremes and allows you to define your workplace purpose in an abbreviated but meaningful format. It's a short statement of your overarching purpose followed by a list of specific outputs you're supposed to deliver. For each item, you note how much of your resources you spend on it, whom you interact with to deliver it, and how your success is measured. Limit the list to between five and seven items to help you achieve some level of detail without creating an overwhelming inventory. You should be able to read it aloud in about 90 seconds.*

Of course, there are many ways to craft such a list. Figure 2.1 shows two examples from individuals with different types of responsibilities at different levels in the same organization. Notice that there are some differences between the lists. The individual worker

*There is an analogy here to the "elevator pitch" concept employed widely by salespeople. The idea is to be able to articulate the value of your offering in the time it takes to ride an elevator with someone so that you and that person can rapidly determine whether further interaction is valuable. Here, the value you describe is your workplace purpose.

expresses resources in terms of his or her time, whereas the manager uses employee effort. The individual is specific in the percentage of time spent on and the project name for each item; the manager is more approximate. And the time frames for outputs differ as well, both between and within the lists. But both lists achieve the same goal: they paint an explicit picture of the output their owner is supposed

FIGURE 2.1 Sample summary outputs lists at different levels of an organization

"I head a department of ten people that ensures that our factory produces high-quality, reliable products. To do that,

- Two of my staff members spend all of their time working on line-yield improvement programs designed to increase our output by at least 12% this year.
- About half of my remaining staff's time is spent reviewing proposed changes to production processes and approving or disapproving them within five days of receipt.
- The other half of my remaining staff's time is split fairly equally among three objectives:
    1. Developing and providing basic factory training to all new employees within 90 days of their hire date
    2. Overseeing specially trained maintenance personnel who conduct audits to ensure our factory is compliant with all quality requirements at all times
    3. Responding within four hours to any factory production issues to ensure that emergency solutions have no impact on output quality over the long term"

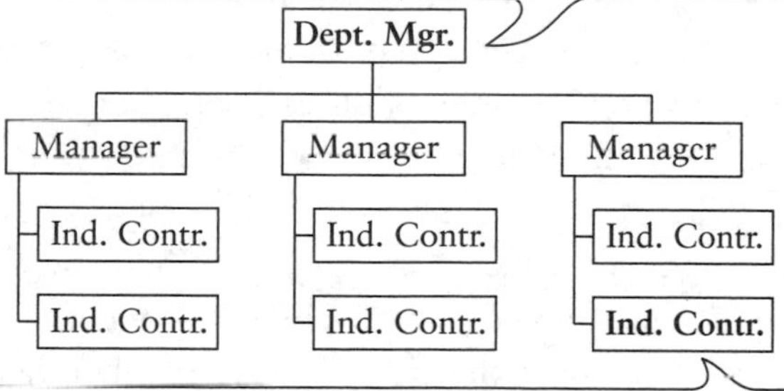

"My purpose is to ensure consistent quality while supporting on-time delivery of output and quality improvement projects. To that end I spend

- 5% of my time reviewing and returning change orders in four hours
- 50% of my time working toward a goal of zero output defects this year
- 25% of my time driving on-time delivery of XYZ in October to mesh with the broader ABC initiative
- 10% of my time troubleshooting business process issues for the quality task force
- 10% of my time driving on-time delivery of Project 123"

Quick Video: Say No Without Saying No

Visit www.MakeWorkGreat.com for a short video segment about how to construct and use a verbalized summary outputs list (VSO) as a statement of your workplace purpose. Note that the video employs the term "verbalized summary ***objectives***" instead of "verbalized summary ***outputs***," but both the acronym and the intent are exactly the same. This is an easy bit of information to share if you're trying to describe the contents of this chapter to a trusted friend or colleague.

to be producing, whether directly or through others. Both capture the elements of the writer's workplace purpose in order of priority and his or her division of resources in appropriate terms. Finally, both have a level of detail that allows them to be meaningful to, memorable to, and easily verbalized by the owner.

That's why in the example no mention is made of revenue or financial return. Summary outputs lists are written in the terms most meaningful to the one doing the work, not to the company. Financial figures are appropriate in lists owned by those at the executive level and by salespeople at all levels, because in those cases financial results are the measure of their output. In most other areas of responsibility it is far preferable to avoid financial figures altogether and instead focus upon the real measurable outcomes that ultimately lead to them.

Notice also what is absent. First, neither list contains any information about *how* the work gets done. There is no mention of time spent talking on the phone, checking e-mail, or traveling. The focus is only on *what* output is needed. Second, both lists omit some of what their owners do. In reality, an endless supply of "additional tasks" lands in everyone's lap. These tangential, potentially distracting jobs are purposely left out to keep the focus on the critical few. Finally, notice that neither list wastes words with contingencies for "if things change." To be sure, things will change. When they do, the lists change to reflect them, and the before-

Be Overt About Your Purpose

WRITE YOUR SUMMARY OUTPUTS

- Don't make assumptions. Delve deep to discover your workplace purpose.
- Write your workplace purpose as a short, overall statement followed by a list of five to seven summary outputs.
- Realize that your list may change frequently and require adjustment.

and-after overtness helps the owner to recognize what's different. The list is a snapshot in time and always subject to revision.

When it comes to workplace purpose, your goal is to become overt about your purpose at the moment, to have a detailed picture of what you're supposed to produce. In doing so, you make your work life easier, pave the way for your other five types of overtness, and write the script that later becomes a platform for communication within your new culture.

2. Be Overt About Your Impact

Behind your workplace purpose lies its impact—the answer to the question "So what?" Perhaps you make a direct contribution to the company's bottom line. Maybe your work supports the efforts of your management team, creates better processes for those around you, or disseminates knowledge. Perhaps your efforts produce a better experience for customers or your work supports a product that saves lives. In any event, the application of your particular expertise to your summary outputs will produce a unique and valuable result. It pays to be open with yourself about that impact.

Consider Brenda, an IT technician in a sales organization. She spent most of her time supporting her company's sales force in the use of customer database, communications, and tracking software. One day, management made a strange request. Sales figures had dipped in the past six months. Her supervisor sent an e-mail asking her to investigate possible causes of the reduction.

At first, Brenda was stymied. She understood why the problem mattered to her company but had no idea how she could help. Was she to interview salespeople and ask them why revenues were down? That wouldn't exactly further her relationship with her internal customers. Should she look into the overall state of the industry and study economic trends? This seemed like a stretch from her area of expertise. She decided to start by talking with a salesperson with whom she had developed a close professional relationship and ask what he would do in her shoes.

His answer was quick and encouraging. Strategic changes in the company's product line had led to smaller up-front capital equipment sales and greater ongoing consumable sales. (Imagine printers that cost less to buy but use more expensive toner.) Revenue calculated by the sales performance software didn't account for consumable sales; these had traditionally been treated as irrelevant. The problem was in the software, and the software was what Brenda knew best. Her potential impact suddenly became obvious.

In a perfect world, the benefit of each of your summary outputs would be self-evident. In reality, overtness will probably be easier for some items than for others. Ask, "What impact can I produce?" or even "Why bother?" for each of your summary outputs and then come up with brief and compelling answers. This will help you understand

Be Overt About Your Impact

ANSWER THE QUESTION "SO WHAT?"

- For each of your summary outputs, determine the beneficial impact when you're successful.
- Articulate that impact in a concise way, using no more than a few sentences.

and quantify your contribution. These same answers also become a compelling set of reasons for your workplace purpose. This can help motivate you and also be useful once you begin to share your summary outputs list with others.

3. Be Overt About Your Incentives

Tanya used to work in the financial sector, overseeing administrative personnel and handling investment policy for the multimillion-dollar portfolio of her publicly held company. Now she works out of her home part-time, providing administrative support to a small, privately owned firm in another industry. She works nearly every weekday but sometimes for only an hour. While her paychecks and her pay rate have both shrunk dramatically, she's happy with the change.

Why? When she left the financial industry, Tanya still wanted to do something that would allow her to be productive and learn new things. She also wanted flexibility to spend time in other pursuits. Because she was overt with herself about those desires, she was able to seek out a position that met her needs perfectly.

Why do you do what you do? The easy answer is survival—"If I didn't work, I'd starve." Your salary, and all it enables you to do, is one incentive. But there are probably other types of work that would allow you to avoid starvation. Did something else originally draw you to this particular industry, company, or position? Was it income potential? Flexibility? Growth and development opportunity? The chance to contribute to society in a broader way? You can probably name some positive aspects of your job, even if you're not terribly

Quick Video: Six Hidden Factors of Motivation

Visit www.MakeWorkGreat.com for a short video segment about six factors that often incentivize us at work. This is also an easy bit of information to share if you're trying to describe the contents of this chapter to a trusted friend or colleague.

Be Overt About Your Incentives

FIGURE OUT WHY

- Consider your salary and the positive things it enables you to do.
- List the most positive or enjoyable aspects of the work involved with your summary outputs.
- Seek opportunities to expand on those positives, even if only slightly.

fond of it. It could be as simple as having a few coworkers you like or as personal as the chance to give back to your community. Or perhaps there's one particular aspect of the work itself that really gives you a charge. Are you an accountant who loves number crunching or a salesperson whose favorite activity is talking to people?*

If so, you have a jump on the third type of overtness—your incentives, or why you want to keep doing what you're doing. These incentives, paycheck included, keep you showing up. If you have enough of them, they also make your workday seem interesting rather than dreadful. Ask yourself, "Why do I work here?" The happier you are at work, the easier the question is to answer. The more miserable you are, the more important it is for you to find out!

Why? First, like Tanya, you can use what motivates you to identify new alternatives. Self-knowledge gives you a filter through which to screen opportunities that come up. Second, once you know what's driving you, you can try to adjust your current work to include a little more of it. Finally, you can focus on those workplace positives when trying to coax yourself out of bed on Monday mornings when you would rather keep sleeping.

---

*One framework for measuring personal motivation suggests that there are six possible motivating factors and that all of us are motivated most strongly by one or two of them; they are to learn, to produce results, to experience harmony, to assist others, to control one's destiny, and to be consistent.[5]

Review your workplace purpose and ask yourself where the positives lie in your own work. Then ask yourself how you might be able to get a little more of what you like.

4. Be Overt About Your Progress

My father had a vivid expression for frustrating days in his workplace. When asked how his day had gone, he would answer that he'd "spent the whole day shoveling sand against the tide." But he used another four-letter word in place of *sand*.

I don't really mind Dad's choice of words, but for this metaphor, I prefer "shoveling sand." I can easily imagine myself in that scene: showing up at the beach in the early morning, shovel in hand; working all day at full capacity, shoveling into the tide; pausing at dusk, breathless and sweaty, and realizing as I look around that nothing has changed. Perhaps this resonates with me a little too well! I have had my share of those days at work, as most of us have.

If you have those days too frequently, you may be missing the fourth kind of overtness: visibility into your progress. It's one thing to have a frustrating and chaotic day or week. But to work constantly without any sense of accomplishment is bad for your morale. No amount of incentive can make up for the hopelessness of shoveling against the tide.

Worse yet, this pattern of work damages productivity. In the new information age workplace, you're surrounded by multiple distractions and requests that divert your attention. If you're unable to perceive progress when you're working toward your workplace purpose, then productive work and distracting work all feel the same. You will lose your ability to filter between what you should be doing and what you should be ignoring, and you'll come to see your workday as an endless line of fires to be put out or tasks to be performed. In a visceral sense, it will cease to matter what you work on, as long as you're busy. This "walk-fast-and-look-worried" type of situation is a recipe for chaos and overload; it's certainly not a way to achieve maximum output with minimum stress.

How can you create overt visibility into your progress? First, focus on just one of the items on your summary outputs list. Visualize yourself having achieved it, and imagine that you are reflecting back on that achievement. Is it a single accomplishment—like a product, physical structure, or report—that you completed at one point in time? Is it a physical or conceptual "stack" of work, such as forms completed or parts assembled, that resulted from your sustained effort? Is it a string of requests or problems, like customer support queries, that you addressed as they arose over time? Get as specific as you can be about what it will look, sound, and feel like to succeed.

Next, consider what will be required of you over each of the next five to seven workdays to achieve that output in the future. If your objective is a report or project, you'll find yourself thinking in terms of small milestones to be reached in the coming week. If your goal is a batch of completed items, you'll be thinking in terms of a processing rate per week, day, and hour. If your output requirement is a group of problems to be solved, you'll imagine your response rate or how quickly you'll solve each one.

Finally, ask yourself the fundamental question for the fourth type of overtness: "How can I make it obvious to myself that I'm making progress?" Ask yourself what progress looks, feels, sounds, and smells like. How do you know, in any given hour of the day, whether you're on track? What can you do to make your progress even more obvious?

Look for answers that require little extra effort on your part and also support the completion of your goals. Perhaps you can turn your small milestones into a checklist of tasks for the day and week that you mark off as you complete them. Maybe you can convert your completion rate per day into an hourly run rate. Or perhaps you can use your problem response rate to develop a personal tracking system for issues as they arise and are solved and in the process begin to notice which ones arise most often.

Seek easy, straightforward approaches. In this case, pen and paper are often preferable to software; simple lists are better than complex plans. For this system to work, it needs to be one that you can use easily. And you won't know that for sure until you put it into practice

Be Overt About Your Progress

CREATE VISIBILITY SYSTEMS

- Imagine the achievement of one of your summary outputs and the appearance and feeling of the result(s).
- Consider what you must complete in the next five to seven workdays to move toward that result.
- Design a simple visibility system that will make it apparent whether you're progressing toward your goal.

and start to actually check off your items or verify your run rate as part of your workday.

Of course, all of this is easier said than done. The specific focus on the appearance of a positive outcome and the deconstruction of that outcome into tangible, incremental steps takes effort, especially if it is a new way of thinking. Rest assured that *difficulty* does not equal *impossibility*. As with most skills, it gets faster and easier with practice. Whatever you do, don't allow yourself to get overwhelmed by the idea of handling all of your summary outputs at once. Remember, your goal is incremental progress; see how well a new system serves you in one area before moving on to another. A little visibility goes a long way.

5. Be Overt About the Resources You Need

A productivity engineer once told me a story about resources that I will never forget. She supported a factory that produced complex parts. Each part was run through multiple pieces of equipment, the most expensive of which cost tens of millions of dollars. As a practical matter, the factory bought as few of the expensive machines as possible, and so had barely enough capacity. When those machines stopped, the factory stopped.

Certain parts needed special processing on the expensive machines. This slower, complicated work was entrusted only to a select group of highly paid expert workers. The goal was to get the special processing done quickly and return the all-important machines to regular work.

However, a resource problem plagued this operation. It was not the multimillion-dollar equipment, the scarce raw material, the expert personnel, or the complex processing information; those were all in plentiful supply. It was a printer. Reaching the small label printer that created the "special processing" tags required a round-trip walk of about 10 minutes. The expert workers, who made this trip at each step in the special processing, were getting paid their expert wage to walk for what amounted to hours each week. Meanwhile, millions of dollars of capital equipment sat idle, all because the company had saved a few hundred dollars by not installing a second printer adjacent to the machines.

Is there a missing label printer in your work life? If so, becoming more overt about resources may be of tremendous value. Three simple questions will help.

The first is whether you have clearly defined the resources you need to complete your summary outputs. Many resources may come into play: your time, other people's time, capital equipment, office supplies, and money, to name a few. You can list the resources required for each of your summary outputs or simply think through what you need. A detailed conceptualization of your requirements is the goal.

The second question is whether the resources you need are available. If you need a forklift or time on a computer, does your employer own one? If you need the support of other people, does your company employ them? The answer may be obvious in some cases, but the question is still worth asking. If you're going to need a resource that isn't available, you need to know.

Finally, you must ask whether you have control of the resources you need. Having money in a budget is one thing; having the authority to spend it the way you need to is quite another. The same is true if your resource list includes time with people or equipment; just because they're out there doesn't mean you'll be able to engage them in the pursuit of your goals.

As Figure 2.2 shows, your answers to all three questions would ideally be affirmative: you know exactly what you need, all resources are available, and you have control over them. Reality is rarely so kind. Most likely, you know most of what you need, the majority of what you need is available, and some of what's available is under your control.

That's why this type of overtness is important. If what you need is not well defined, then you need to return to your summary outputs and seek answers there. If what you need is not available, awareness of that problem will cause you to pursue alternatives or adjust your

FIGURE 2.2 Ideal versus actual resource conditions

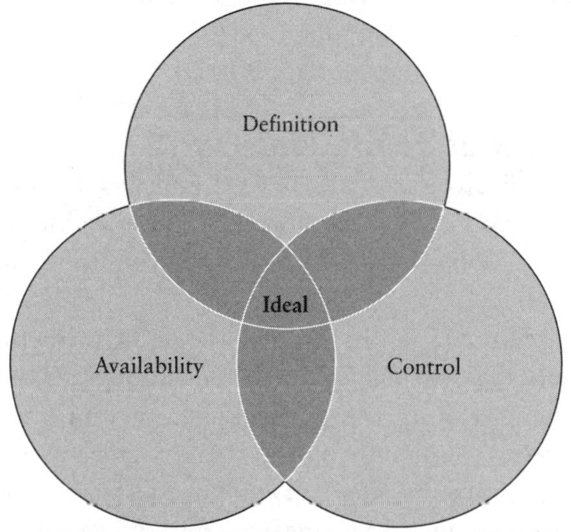

Be Overt About the Resources You Need

DEFINE NEED, AVAILABILITY, AND CONTROL

- Use your summary outputs list to define the resources you need.
- Determine whether those resources are available; note which are not.
- Determine which of the available resources you control and which you don't.

output plan accordingly. And if what you need is not under your control, your knowledge of that fact will guide you to seek influence.

Overtness about resources can be particularly helpful when you notice (thanks to visibility systems) that you have ceased to make progress, but you aren't sure why. For now, of course, you're just practicing. Simply consider your resources and note the concerns you uncover so you can revisit them later.

6. Be Overt About Your Capability

Can you know what you don't know? Careful, it's a trick question. To know whether you know what you don't know would require you to know what you don't know, which is what you don't know if you know. You know?

The semantics are offered in jest, but the point is important. The early information-age workplace is in a constant state of flux. The information flying around the network—the crystalline structure defined in Chapter 1—isn't moving in a vacuum. It's having impact as it goes! A new court ruling alters an employee absence policy; a nugget of marketplace intelligence changes a new product release; a bit of manufacturability data from production adjusts the plan for the next version of a product. Changes are constant.

More often than not, impacts are subtle. Maybe the written employee absence policy doesn't change, but the preferred response to absences is made more or less severe within existing guidelines. Perhaps the new product schedule doesn't change, but marketplace positioning does. Maybe the next generation design doesn't change, but new manufacturing approaches are considered. Placed in the right hands, every meaningful bit of information represents a question. Every question has many possible answers, most of which suggest a change. The easiest and therefore most frequent changes are made without adjusting formal doctrine or written policies and procedures, and the quasi-informal communication of such changes only adds to the complexity and information overload we all face.

Even as changes occur, more new information appears, which raises more questions. Changes beget new information; new information begets changes. As you learn more about your situation, you share your knowledge; as you share your knowledge, it changes others' situations too. In the information network, every person is both producer and recipient. Tapping into this information as it flies around the network and feeding back the right information in return are critical parts of nearly every job.

Of course, the information "out there" is only half of the story. Equally important is the question of whether you have the skills to do your work. Which skills do you need? The answer changes along with everything else. And if peering out at the information network is difficult, looking inward at your own strengths and weaknesses can be nearly impossible. We have been taught by our parents, schools, interviewers, supervisors, and political leaders that we must always appear to know exactly what we're doing. But sometimes we don't!

The sixth form of overtness, being overt about your capability, is a way of gaining insight about both the information "out there" and the skills you have "in here." To develop this overtness, you must consider both parts of Figure 2.3 and the relationship between them.

First, consider the sensitivities of your summary outputs. What other people, groups, departments, or divisions can set policies that

FIGURE 2.3 The two components of capability

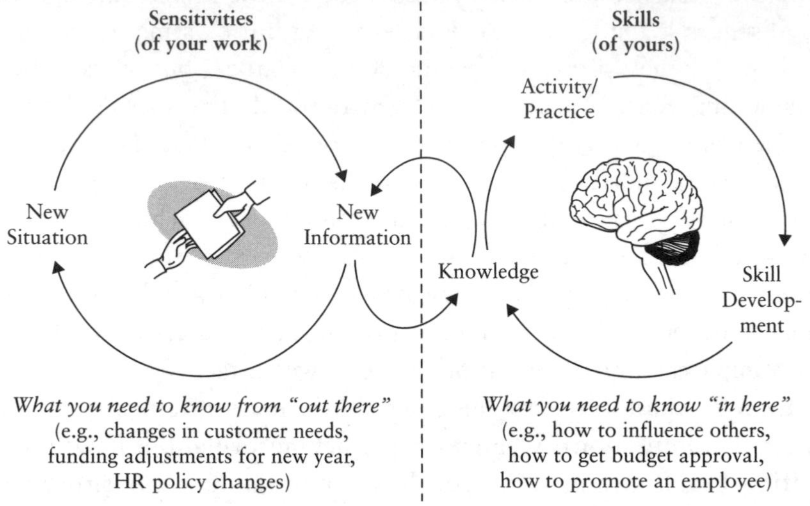

affect your work? These could be inside or outside your organization—superiors, subordinates, customers, or support groups. Most likely, your summary outputs share some sensitivities. As a manager, for example, nearly everything you do will be impacted by employee management guidelines set by human resources.

Next, consider the skills involved in each of your summary objectives. What hard skills—factual, process, or technical knowledge—do you need? What soft skills—interpersonal, conceptual, or execution-related abilities—do you require? Some come directly from the work; others flow from changes on the sensitivities side. In assessing your own skills, objectivity is important. You may find it helpful to imagine you're training a friend to take over your workplace purpose, as a way of removing some of your personal bias.

Finally, ponder who might help bring you more information in each area. Which coworkers have insight into the sensitivities you've identified? Whom do you know who can comment honestly about your skills? Maybe you have a friend in human resources or a close contact at a customer site who can tell you about new policies; perhaps

Be Overt About Your Capability

KNOW WHAT YOU NEED TO KNOW

- Determine the sensitivities of each of your summary outputs: what individuals or groups can make changes that impact your goals?
- Consider the skills you need to deliver on each of your summary objectives: what do you need to know how to do?
- Identify people and/or tools that can help you answer these questions.

you have a relationship with a coworker, employee, or manager that allows for an honest discussion of your strengths. Make note of both groups of people; they are key sources of information regarding the sixth form of overtness.

If you lack people in either category, consider your alternatives. For example, "360-degree feedback," the increasingly common structured process of seeking input from coworkers at all levels, can provide useful insight into your strengths and weaknesses if managed correctly. Or you may decide to work toward forging some relationships with people who can give you the information you need. Does your company have a mentoring program? Is there a good personal coach in your organization or your community, perhaps one who uses objective assessment tools? Ultimately, there's no substitute for the honesty and objectivity of someone who knows about the sensitivities and skills related to your work—or who knows how to discover them.*

---

*As a former engineer, I recommend and use only 360-degree or self-reporting assessment tools that meet high standards for analytical rigor (validity, face validity, normative population size, etc.). I encourage others to use the same approach when considering possible tools. The wide variety of options available can make the selection process daunting, but the effort is worthwhile. The quality of the information you receive is only as good as the technique or instrument you employ, and irrelevant, incomplete, or incorrect information about one's own skills can be wasteful and damaging on many levels when it is presented as being factual.

For now, focus only on finding new information. What do you know, and how might you open doors to discover more?

It's a Lot, and It's a Little

As you can see, all six forms of overtness help you address that critical ratio: your level of output and the amount of stress around you. By being overt with yourself about what you're supposed to deliver, the impact of those deliveries on your "customers," your incentives for making the deliveries, how you're progressing, and what resources and information you need to make your deliveries, you begin to build a workplace for yourself in which you know exactly what you're doing and how you're doing it. You begin to focus not only on maximum output, but also on minimum stress.

If much of this is new to you, don't make the mistake of trying to do everything at once. Start small and build from there. If all you do this week is create a more complete summary outputs list for yourself, it will be an excellent first step. If all you do in the subsequent two weeks is create a visibility system for just one of your outputs, that's plenty. Small, regular steps in the right direction are far preferable to a flurry of activity followed by a stall.

As you begin to improve on your own six types of overtness, you'll notice improvements in your critical ratio. You'll see more output with less stress. This is not only an enhancement to your own work but also the start of the seed crystal for the new culture you plan to grow. Nucleation has begun.

EXERCISES

1. Review the six types of overtness about task.

2. Write a summary outputs list for your job or set a date by which you will do so. Include an overall purpose statement and five

to seven specific objectives that comprise the majority of what you're supposed to deliver.

---

3. Set goals to work on one or two types of overtness for one or two of your summary outputs in the following few weeks. Table 2.1 may prove helpful in organizing your thoughts and plans. It can also serve as the table of contents for the notebook you started in Chapter 1. Begin by setting a deadline by which you will have crafted a first draft of your summary outputs statements; write this deadline in column 1. Then select one of the individual items on your summary outputs list and select one area of overtness from columns 2 through 6. Set a deadline for you to explore only that area of overtness, for only that item on your summary outputs list. Write it in the appropriate location in the table. Never set more than two such deadlines at a time, and don't set new deadlines until old items are completed. This will help you to make small, incremental improvement in your level of overtness without becoming overwhelmed.

TABLE 2.1 Six Types of Overtness: Personal Planning Table

	1. Be Overt About Your Purpose	2. Be Overt About Your Personal Impact	3. Be Overt About Your Incentives	4. Be Overt About Your Progress	5. Be Overt About the Resources You Need	6. Be Overt About Your Capability
Summary Output 1:	Write summary outputs by ______	Impact statement by ______	Incentives list by ______	Visibility system by ______	Resource list by ______	Sensitivities and skills list by ______
Summary Output 2:		Impact statement by ______	Incentives list by ______	Visibility system by ______	Resource list by ______	Sensitivities and skills list by ______
Summary Output 3:		Impact statement by ______	Incentives list by ______	Visibility system by ______	Resource list by ______	Sensitivities and skills list by ______
Summary Output 4:		Impact statement by ______	Incentives list by ______	Visibility system by ______	Resource list by ______	Sensitivities and skills list by ______

3 Clarity Within Relationships

If you're like most people, thinking through the six types of overtness probably led you to some uncomfortable realizations.

- You may have realized that the person who writes your performance review and controls your pay would probably not understand or agree with parts of your summary outputs list (a problem with purpose).
- You may have had the depressing realization that too much of your workplace effort goes toward no seemingly pertinent result (a problem with impact).
- Perhaps you were faced with the unpleasant notion that much of what motivated you to take your present job in the first place has changed (a problem with incentives).
- You may have come to the painful conclusion that although you work as hard as you can all day, things haven't changed because of it, at least not that you can see (a problem with visibility into progress).
- Maybe it became obvious that something you really need to accomplish your workplace purpose is not well defined, is not available, or is out of your control (a problem with resources).

- Perhaps you have gained a new level of insight into how little you know relative to how much you're expected to accomplish (a problem with capability).

Faced with unpleasant discoveries like these, you may have been tempted to divert your attention elsewhere. Forget about overtness! Turn off the light, close the door, and leave the skeleton in the closet where you found it. Put down the troublesome book that's causing you to question things best left unexamined and get back to your daily grind.

Or you may have latched onto your depressing new discovery with miserable glee. "*This* is the reason my job is so messed up," you exclaim. "*This* is the reason it can never get better!" Perhaps you're already making plans to share your newfound bit of hopelessness with your coworkers. "I'm reading this book that says it's supposed to be this way, and it's not. Now I know why things will never improve."

Unfortunately, neither ignoring nor complaining about the difficulties you uncover is particularly beneficial to your output-stress ratio—not if you want to create a culture change, and not even if you just want a slightly better workplace. So try hard not to be too surprised, mortified, frightened, paralyzed, or aggravated at what you discover. Just remember that the discovery of each problem is the first step in its resolution.

The next step, of course, is to look for answers.

Seeking Clarity

The act of seeking clarity is well understood and widely practiced by those most adept at negotiating the early information age workplace. It is the searching out of viable answers to the ever-present questions constantly raised by your complex work.

It begins with a simple but important assumption: conflicts, constraints, confusion, and complexity are facts of life. Their presence does not represent the failure of an employee to handle work correctly, the failure of a manager to assign work properly, or the failure of a leadership team to "make life easier." They are not your fault, and they are not "their" fault. They simply exist as a natural product of today's workplace.

Let's pause for an important aside. The *amount* of conflicts, constraints, confusion, and complexity is often a direct result of the employees, managers, and leaders involved. Incompetent workers, clueless managers, and disconnected leaders certainly add to the problem by making things harder than they need to be, and such people should be held accountable. But that performance management conversation, albeit an important one, is for another time. In the context of seeking clarity, we just accept that these stressors will be there, no matter how good or bad our managers and employees are. Rather than trying to assign blame for these issues, we merely note them as a value-neutral reality, one that has been, is, and always will be with us at work.

Seeking clarity is the simple act of looking for next steps while accepting that some chaos is inevitable; it is about moving forward anyway. It's not concerned with discovering permanent, perfect, universal solutions that eliminate conflicts, constraints, confusion, and complexity, because it recognizes that such solutions don't exist. Instead, it's an intention to discover or create simple, immediate, realistic answers to the question of what to do at the moment.

Emma, my former manager and favorite expert in crystal building (from Chapter 1), was quite adept at this behavior. I'm certain it wasn't easy. Imagine yourself in her shoes: a senior leader whose organization's problems are costing the company millions of dollars a day in lost revenue. Would you be tempted to put hard pressure on the person responsible? Would you want to tell your new employee that he'd better figure things out or get packing? Would you be inclined to throw six more senior people at the problem out of sheer desperation? I know I would. But Emma knew better. She sought clarity from those who understood something about the problem—myself included—and determined that the solution required not more people, but more time. She sought clarity from me as to what I needed to make headway, and she took action based on my needs instead of her fears. At the same time, she sought clarity from other interested parties about what was happening and why. In the process, she put them at ease, solicited their help when necessary, and kept them out of my way. Most of Emma's contributions over the life of the problem could actually be characterized as either the act or product of seeking clarity. It was the core of all she did.

Seeking clarity is the art of soliciting the information you need to decide your most intelligent next move, given that many things still remain undetermined. But it's more than just walking around asking about what's happening. To effectively seek clarity, you must prepare specific definitions for three things: the question you're asking, the approach you'll take in asking it, and the specific need for agreement that it entails.

1. Define Your Question

As you consistently practice the six types of overtness from Chapter 2 and struggle with the inevitable questions they raise, you'll find yourself needing answers in order to move forward. Defining your questions clearly is the first step in finding those answers. As you read the examples of well-defined questions that follow (organized around the six types of overtness), think about which of them best apply to you today. After all, whatever your job in the crystalline network may be, your first priority is to discover and define that job.

First and foremost are questions that pertain to purpose, and they are designed to help clarify your summary outputs list. Your questions in this area may sound something like this:

- What exactly am I trying to accomplish?
- Who is involved with my output requirements?
- How should I spend my time and resources?
- Which of my activities are most important?

Here, you're seeking clarity about your role in the network. Imagine having a conversation with your boss about one of your goals, such as improving sales performance. You may start out trying to agree on your success criteria and, in the process, discover that the two of you are analyzing sales data differently. The next question—how do we calculate the results?—may turn out to be the most important one of all.

The second set of questions is about your impact. These are the "whys" behind your objectives:

- How will the results I produce benefit the recipient?
- How will my work produce positive impact for my coworkers or customers?
- What contribution am I making?
- Will I be able to tell that I've made a contribution?

In discussions about impact, you clarify the value you deliver to the network. A conversation with a customer about what he or she really wants may lead quickly to new understanding about what you need to do. Perhaps you were hired to provide a product, but your unspoken role is to give your customers peace of mind (a service of sorts). To be successful, you need to clearly understand both components.

Third, consider your incentives. Here, you might ask questions like these:

- What do I gain from doing this work?
- What do I enjoy about it?
- What parts of it bring me pleasure?
- Why did I agree to do this?

In this case, you're seeking reasons to stay in the network. This consideration is often overlooked, but notice how important it is: every moment of every day, you choose whether to remain in the network or disconnect from it. From that decision flows the energy you use to maintain and strengthen your communication links. It's critically important for you to be clear that you *are* choosing to stay and *why* you're choosing to stay. The answers may come from you, a manager, a mentor, or even a family member. But they must come from somewhere. "Half in, half out" is a recipe for disaster (not to mention despair).

Fourth, turn your attention to visibility into your progress. Consider these questions:

- How do I know I'm making progress?
- How can I be sure I'm working on the right things?
- What confidence do I have that I'll meet my commitments?
- How often am I correct when I estimate my own completion time?

These questions raise the issue of the rate at which you're creating in the network. You might talk with a colleague who has a role similar to yours and compare notes regarding your personal monitoring processes. Or you might seek the counsel of a mentor who has done your job in the past and learn how he or she tracked progress.

Fifth are questions concerned with the resources you need:

- What materials or resources do I require?
- What funding will I need?
- Are the materials, resources, and funding available (that is, do they exist)?
- Do I have control over the materials, resources, and funding? If not, who does?

Here, you focus on what you need from the network and how you will get it. You might seek to negotiate with a fellow manager for the time and assistance of one of his direct reports on one of your projects. While the starting point for the conversation might be a request for help, it may turn out that the two of you manage employee resource sharing in dissimilar ways, so a broader conversation about the negotiation processes between you would be valuable.

Finally come questions about your capability:

- What functional knowledge do I have about how things work?
- What knowledge do I need?

Define Your Question

DECIDE IN ADVANCE WHAT MUST BE DISCUSSED

- Consider which of the six types of overtness generated the question or concern you need answered.
- Use the samples in this section for reference as you articulate your question as specifically as possible.

- Which of my interpersonal or conceptual skills are strong?
- How do the skills I already have relate to the skills I need?

In this case, you're asking what knowledge you contribute to the network. You could easily ask these questions of a manager, a mentor, and a customer, and you'd receive very different answers. Perhaps your boss would say that you most need to have "influencing skills," but the customer would advise you to focus on your "technical problem-solving" abilities.

As you can see from all of these examples, having a set of well-defined questions is critical when you're seeking clarity. Write them down if you can. Definition of questions is the first step. Stay flexible! You may uncover a direct answer quickly, you may slowly develop a solution, or you may learn something along the way that causes you to redefine entirely what you're seeking. No matter how things turn out, by keeping an eye on what you're looking for, you improve your chances of finding it.

2. Define Your Approach

On the surface, it seems that once you have your questions defined, you're done. "I know what I need to know," you may be saying. "Now it's time to go find out." If you have this impulse to seek answers from the crystalline network around you, congratulations, it's a good one. But before you head off armed with your questions, you need to consider the approach you intend to take. More specifically, you must consider to whom you plan to speak first, what you'll talk about, and how you plan to approach that person.

Start with who you see as the right person for your discussion. If your question is well defined, one or more possible individuals will often be apparent. If you need clarity regarding your purpose or impact, it will typically come from someone who manages you or someone who receives your output. If you need clarity about your incentives or a better visibility system to monitor your progress, it may come from your peers or perhaps a mentor. If you need clarity about your resources or capability, you might choose to solicit information or feedback from your employees or from trusted associates within your professional network. These ideas are no substitute for your own expertise, of course; you know better than anyone where to start your search for answers. Get specific, and name one or two people who are most likely to help you answer your question.

Next comes what you plan to say. Obviously you have a question. But there's a difference between having a question and asking a question. Remember that you can seek an answer honestly without asking the question directly.

Imagine for a moment that an employee you're managing or a member of a team you're leading visits you. He has been working for you for some time, and you're generally happy with his work. Today, he wants to talk about his workplace purpose. Consider two different tacks he might take:

> *Conversation starter 1: "I don't think I fully understand my responsibility for outputs to you and our team. Can you please tell me what you expect from me?"*

Or,

> *Conversation starter 2: "I've been working under the assumption that my primary responsibilities to you involve publishing current*

progress updates to the team every Friday and providing answers within a day to business process questions that are presented to me by our team members. I'd like to confirm with you that I have a correct and complete understanding of what you expect from me."

In the first option, this person is putting you on the spot. In the best possible case, you're ready with a clear answer and you give it. Even so, there may be a part of you that is disappointed in him; it sounds as though he hasn't known what he was supposed to be doing until now! In the worst case, you don't have a meaningful response on the tip of your tongue. That puts you in an even more difficult position. Do you tell him you're not sure or ask him to wait for an answer while you check your notes? That sends a signal that what he's doing isn't that important, which could disappoint and demoralize him. Do you feel a little defensive, embarrassed that you *should* know the answer? If so, he may pick up on your nervous energy and become nervous himself. Or do you throw the question back at him, asking, "Why don't you tell me what you think you're supposed to be doing?" That gets you out of the hot seat and puts him in it, but it doesn't help with any real information exchange.

The second option is much easier on you, as the receiver of the request. Your team member presented his current understanding of his summary outputs as a platform for discussion. He shared his understanding of his primary goals and gave you a starting point to agree or disagree with them. You're much less likely to feel defensive because you're not being questioned, and you're much less likely to make him feel defensive because he has invited your edits to his understanding. Nobody is demoralized, and nobody is disappointed. This approach has a much better chance of leading to the exchange of information that was its original goal.

In preparing to find answers to your own questions, consider taking a conversational approach like your fictitious employee's second alternative. What you talk about should include your current understanding of the answer to your question and an invitation to the other person to edit that understanding.

Quick Video: Smart Managers Read Behavior

Visit www.MakeWorkGreat.com for a short video segment about how to define the pace and content of your approach to another person. This is also an easy bit of information to share if you're trying to describe the contents of this chapter to a trusted friend or colleague. Although it is directed primarily at managers, its lessons work equally well for anyone at any level who is attempting to communicate with another person.

Once you have determined who you'll talk to and what you'll talk about, it's time to consider how you'll interact with the other person. This powerful aspect of approach is often overlooked. Everyone in our new information age workplace carries a heavy load and is burdened with his or her own responsibilities. With every dialogue you initiate, you're asking for someone else's time and attention. This is their most valuable commodity! How you approach that conversation can increase or decrease your chances of being heard and getting helped by the person whose counsel you have decided to seek.

There's only one rule here, and it is as simple as it is meaningful. Whatever conversation you intend to have, whatever issue you plan to raise, whatever question you plan to ask, frame it for the benefit of the other person. In other words, be prepared to converse not in the way that is most natural for you, but in the way that is most natural for him or her. Two simple guidelines can be tremendously beneficial here.[1]

First, be ready to match the other person's pace. If he or she is someone who walks, talks, and moves quickly, plan on a quick interaction. Make sure your statement of your current understanding is concise, and be ready to have a rapid discussion toward a rapid answer. If he or she is a more reflective, more thoughtful type, then prepare a more thorough statement at the outset and have backup information ready if you're asked for it. Expect more requests for clarification, and be prepared to leave the person time to think and ponder before getting back to you with an answer. If you're not sure which approach is best, then prepare in both ways and be ready to switch gears if the situation warrants.

Define Your Approach

PREPARE THE WHO, WHAT, AND HOW OF YOUR INTERACTION

- Who: decide which person you plan to approach for an answer to your well-defined question.
- What: determine a way to open the conversation by inviting edits to your current understanding, rather than simply asking an open-ended question.
- How: plan how you'll pace the interaction and how much attention you'll give to issues of task and deadline versus people and relationships so you can match the other person's tendencies.

Second, prepare to focus on the same elements of conversation as the other person. If your target is someone who tends to discuss tasks, projects, facts, and deadlines, then be ready to discuss those issues. Or if you know that he or she usually takes a keen interest in the people and human relationships involved, prepare yourself to discuss those topics. Again, if you're unsure as to which way things will go, prepare both aspects well so that you can go in whatever direction the ultimate discussion calls for.

As you can see, the three aspects of your approach—who, what, and how—are worthy of your time and consideration. They are also worth putting down on paper. By defining your approach in writing, you're preparing your interaction—a link in your network—to be as effective as possible. Now you not only have a burning question but an avenue through which to find an answer.

3. Define Your Need for Agreement

The last step in seeking clarity is to define your need for agreement. Even with a well-defined question and a carefully thought-out approach, the issue of agreement can be a huge stumbling block—and a tremendous distraction—when it comes to seeking clarity. Often, whether or not two people agree becomes the primary topic of their conversation and overshadows the original topic of discussion and all the preparations they made. Consider this simple dialogue between two managers:

ANN: Thank you, Gina, for sharing one of your team members for the past eight weeks to support the systems improvement project I'm leading. It looks like we're going to need him for one more week to finish things out. My understanding from our original plan was that this amount of overrun wouldn't be a problem, but I wanted to confirm that with you now.

GINA: As you know, I've always had my doubts about that project. I agree with the need, but are you sure we're taking the right approach?

ANN: Well, I can understand your doubts, but our research supports the conclusions we've drawn and the direction we're taking.

GINA: I heard about that research, but I don't know that it included an appropriate sample of information.

ANN: We were careful to include multiple population samples. Let me list them for you . . .

And so on.

Is there anything wrong with this exchange? Perhaps not. Ann opens with a statement of her current understanding of the answer to her question and an invitation to edit it. Gina expresses what may be appropriate related questions. Ann appears to have the answers and is willing to share them. This might turn out to be an interesting conversation. The chance to share information may produce better alignment between the two managers and even serve to improve the trust between them on a personal level.

On the other hand, this may also be a rehash of an old argument. Perhaps Ann and Gina have a long-standing disagreement regarding this project, and today's conversation is just the next in a series of endless debates. Or perhaps either or both are busy with other priorities and simply don't have the time for this extended conversation.

The exchange might leave both feeling misunderstood and frustrated with each other and end up damaging their relationship.

The important point here is not to determine whether the outcome of the conversation will be "good" or "bad" but to realize that the topic of conversation has shifted because of an unstated assumption. Ann started out seeking clarity regarding a specific resource question: one extra week of an employee's time. But the dialogue quickly turned into a discussion about the value of the project. The subtle but important twist is that both managers began acting as though they were required to agree over the value of the project in order to make a decision about the shared resource. Both Ann and Gina did what felt natural: they went where the conversation led them. Unfortunately, it led them away from the real point of needed clarity.

Ann's question was well defined, but she would have benefited from defining her need for agreement at the outset. She needed to be clear—with herself at least, and probably with Gina as well—that the only agreement she needed was about the extra week of the employee's time. Any agreement beyond that simply wasn't necessary. Imagine what would happen if her last line in the preceding dialogue were replaced with this one:

> **ANN:** We were careful to include multiple population samples, and I have data that we could go over if you like. But we seem to be switching topics. For the moment, perhaps we can agree to disagree about the overall value of the project and return to my original question about borrowing your team member next week. Is there any reason that would be a problem?

Agreeing to disagree is a powerful tool when it comes to seeking clarity. Clarity is often different from agreement, as in this case. Whether or not Ann and Gina choose to have the conversation about the value of Ann's project, and whether or not they ultimately agree on that value, the question of resource sharing still requires its own clarity. Ann's original question—"Can I have your employee's help for one more week?"—is a valid one, which she needs answered so she can move forward.

Agreeing to disagree can manifest itself in many productive ways in the workplace. Here are a few examples:

- One manager can share resources with another in support of the greater goals of the company without agreeing over every detail of the second manager's project or how it will be run (agreement on need or goal does not require agreement on strategy or tactics).
- Two ordinarily independent salespeople with different approaches to customer interaction can agree to follow a specific approach together when partnering on a large, complex client call (agreement on the best approach to one specific client does not require agreement on the best approach to all clients).
- Two engineers with strong, conflicting notions about the appropriate way to analyze a set of production-line fault data can agree to run both analyses and look for common, actionable conclusions rather than to argue over which approach to take (practical agreement on the need for a quick solution does not require philosophical agreement on how to get there).
- Two coworkers with different personal or political beliefs can set those aside at work to produce output for the good of their mutual employer (agreement regarding workplace output does not require agreement of political or personal beliefs).

This sort of clarity sounds simple on paper, but it can be tricky in the middle of a complex interaction. Our tendency is to go where the conversation leads us, especially when another person is asking us a question. Without having clearly defined our need for agreement in advance, it's far too easy to get derailed.

Since it's easier on paper, do it on paper! You have your question defined, and you have a plan for your approach (who, what, and how). Now write down a clear definition of the exact agreement you need from that individual. This way you can keep your focus where it belongs, even when the momentum of a complex conversation tries to take you somewhere else.

Define Your Need for Agreement

SEEK THE LEAST AMOUNT OF AGREEMENT NECESSARY

- Clarify what agreement you need from the other person.
- Think about what issues may arise and where it would be appropriate to agree to disagree.

At this point, you should be feeling well prepared. You're seeking clarity in a way that is most likely to produce a successful result, both in terms of finding the answer you need and in terms of making the process painless for you and the other person involved.

The Network Is the Workplace

As we near the end of the first section of this book, it seems clear that we're running out of ways to discuss you and your work without also talking about the people with whom you interact.

That's no coincidence. Recall our abstract representation of the early information age workplace, a network of nodes and links. You and the people around you are the nodes, and the communication paths between you are the links. This crystalline network extends infinitely in all directions, but you naturally only have visibility into the part of it closest to you, the part that you can metaphorically "see." From your perspective, you're somewhere near the center of your irregular crystal, which extends beyond your perception.

Figure 3.1 is not difficult to conceptualize as an interactive model. You can easily imagine those you interact with most frequently—whether they are customers, managers, employees, colleagues, or anyone else—as being nearer to you in the crystalline network, with others being farther away. The people on the edge of your personal crystal are those with whom you have less interaction; you probably have less insight into their roles and constraints.

FIGURE 3.1 Your place in the crystalline node/network model

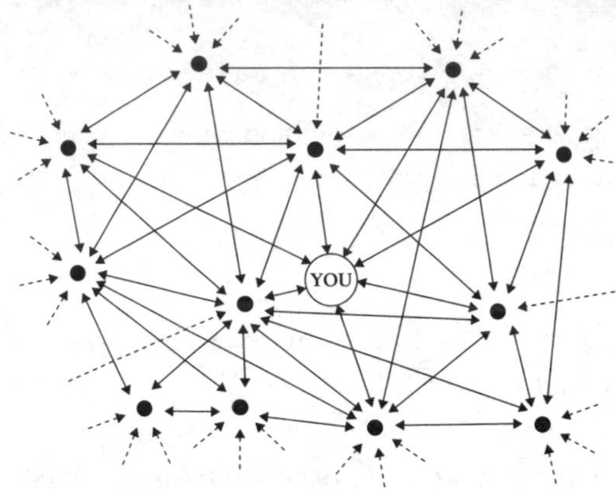

Despite this visual representation, it can be difficult to think about this crystalline network as the single source of your entire workplace experience, including your productivity, your enjoyment, your problems, and your solutions.

Consider this. In the mid-1980s, John Gage of Sun Microsystems made a compelling statement about the future of computing that is still the visionary basis for the company today. He said, "The network is the computer."[2] At the time, this was an alien concept to the majority of computer users, who could each see their computer and count on their fingers the small number of outside services to which it could connect. The computer was the computer, and the network wasn't much. Today, Gage's visionary statement is making a lot more sense. With the advent of on-demand Internet-based services of all kinds for individuals and businesses of all sizes, the computer on your desk is more than the machine doing the work; it's the access portal to the system that does it.

The change in the role of the worker is no different. In the early information age workplace, we are no longer a collection of semi-isolated individuals completing neat bundles of work in a vacuum and passing along our output to the next step. We are not links in a single chain. Instead, each of us works on an interrelated piece of a broader puzzle. Our assignments come in from the crystalline network; they are shaped and changed by it as we go. Our work involves others in the network, and our output, when it's ready, is delivered to multiple points in the network. Each of us is not only a machine doing the work, but also an interface to the broader system that does it.

So the crystalline network in Figure 3.1 is far more than an inventory of who you spend your time talking to. It is, as a whole, the driver of your role, your activity, and your output at work. It is the environment that creates your work and the environment you create through your work, all in one.

The network is the manager. The network is the customer. The network is the coworker. The network is the workplace.

Your Network Upgrade

Let's be clear. When we talk about "the crystalline network," we're not talking about a geological item purchased at a new age bookstore and hung in your entryway to help balance invisible forces. We're simply speaking of a system of people, or nodes, and the communication paths, or links, between them. You represent one node; your connection to the network is simply the quantity and quality of your links. Those links are the paths between you and those who are figuratively around you in your structure.

We have defined two "network competencies" so far in this book: being overt about your tasks, and seeking clarity within your relationships when your overtness raises questions. Hopefully, it's becoming apparent that these competencies are more than just general notions of what to talk about with your colleagues. They're an interrelated pair of disciplines that together comprise the way in which you wire yourself to your workplace.

The act of being overt raises questions; the act of seeking clarity provides answers. Every answer raises questions, and every question suggests answers. The repetition of the question/answer cycle

FIGURE 3.2 The overtness/clarity or question/answer cycle

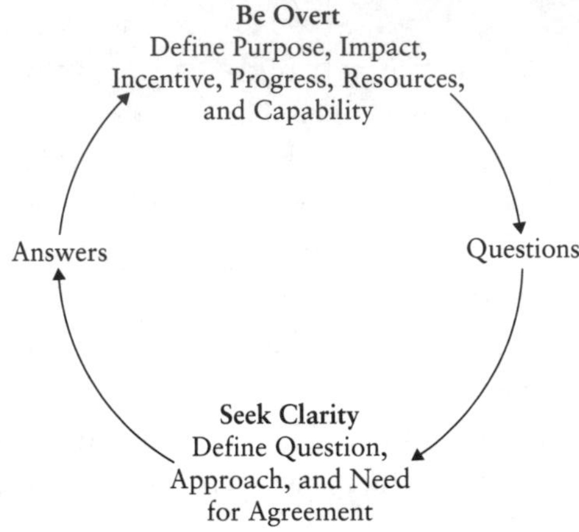

in Figure 3.2 strengthens your connection to the network. It literally changes what you work on and how you work on it, improving your ability to produce output. It's like upgrading from a dial-up to a broadband Internet connection on your home computer. You may not have changed the information "out there," but you have dramatically improved your ability to use it to produce results.

Tasks, Relationships, Tasks, Relationships

You may have noticed—with delight or despair—that there is a higher-level cycle at play here. To get the answers you need to complete your tasks, you seek clarity from the people around you. To maintain positive relationships with those people, you need to be perceived as capable, honest, and trustworthy. In other words, you need to complete your tasks.

The result can be a vicious cycle, as shown in Figure 3.3. To successfully complete your tasks, you need strong relationships; to maintain strong relationships, you must successfully complete your tasks. If you struggle with either, you struggle with both.

FIGURE 3.3 Tasks and relationships: a vicious circle?

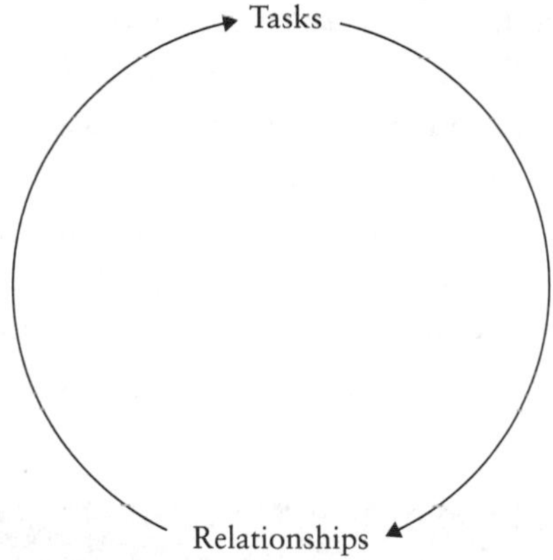

Unemployed suburban teenagers who have just reached driving age know all about vicious cycles. To get a car, they need money from a job. To get a job, they need a car to get there. At first glance, the problem seems unsolvable, but countless teens solve it every year. How? By keeping both in balance and working on both simultaneously. Borrow Mom's car, work a few hours, beg or borrow a little family money, buy a cheap car, get a steadier job, get a better car, and so on. With effort and patience, even a "stuck," or downward, spiral can be converted to an upward one. The secret is to place your focus not on one element or the other, but on maintaining balance between them both.

As you constantly balance output with stress, completion of a task is sometimes most important; other times, relationships take precedence. Is it more important to get your boss to clarify his policy further or to give him the sense that you can be trusted to do what's necessary without asking questions? Is it better to mandate overtime so your employees finish extra work this quarter or to allow them extra time off to spend the holidays with family? Is it preferable to handle a minor attendance issue with leniency or with strictness? The answer is different every time, and the question must constantly be asked, answered, and asked again.

That's Enough About You

We close the first section of this book with a complete definition of your personal node in the crystalline network. By being overt about the tasks you must perform, you raise questions; by seeking clarity through your relationships, you find answers. In the process, by balancing your attention between the tasks on your plate and your relationships with others, you make improvements in both areas.

This overall balance—between tasks and relationships, between questions and answers, between being overt and seeking clarity—is your solution to the problem of maximizing output while minimizing

Stress in the Crystalline Network

The mandate of the early information age workplace is to make more decisions, more quickly, based upon more information than ever before. Yet, studies have concluded that in the absence of coping mechanisms, time pressure adversely impacts the ability of decision makers to consider and weigh competing information appropriately, make accurate judgments, and consider multiple alternatives.[3] Subsequent research adds ambiguity to the list of decision-making stressors and confirms that such stressors reduce the opportunity to gather information, process it, and give undivided attention to the task at hand.[4] And dividing attention is itself problematic: research suggests that the task-switching involved in such "multitasking" uses valuable time and cognitive processing power.[5]

In light of this, it's easy to see how decision making and stress can create a downward spiral—of information overload, ambiguity, time pressure, and stress—that leads to decreased output and engagement. Perhaps worst of all, the spiral accelerates itself naturally, because even the anticipation of future stressful events can have the same cognitive impact as actual stressors![6] Eliminating that spiral and replacing it with coping mechanisms in the form of an optimized balance between output and stress is the key to survival and growth in the crystalline workplace; it's the key to making work great.

FIGURE 3.4 Your node in the crystalline network

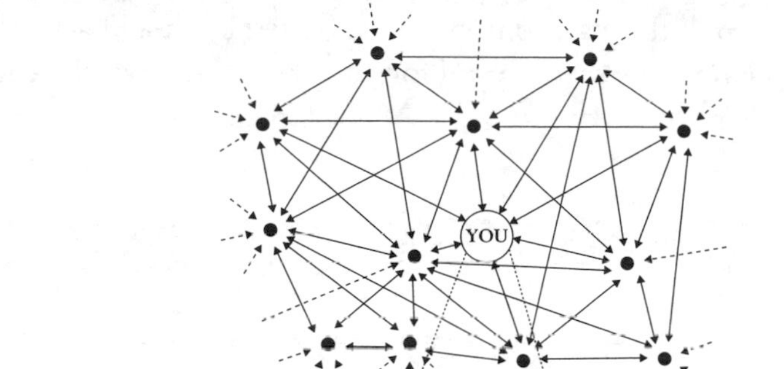

stress. It is the core of your strategy for accomplishing your work in a way that is both effective in the moment and sustainable over the long term. As you can see from Figure 3.4, the output-stress ratio is at the center of your balancing act.

Is it now obvious why an entire section of this book is dedicated to your node? The balance you strike here determines not only how productive you are, but also how you are perceived by those around you in your network. In the early information age workplace, we are all connected, which means we are all on stage. The way in which you maintain your balance is your individual marketing campaign, your announcement to the network about what you value and how you do things. It is also your own set of precedents, the unspoken tactics you employ today that become the culture around you tomorrow. When you are successful and your cycle spirals upward, your success becomes a real-life infomercial about how things should be done. In a nutshell (or perhaps a node-shell), it is what you demonstrate to other people by your actions and, through your example, how they should act.

This is—you are—the seed crystal for your reinvention of the culture. This is where you begin to Make Work Great.

EXERCISES

1. Review the three types of clarity within relationships.

2. Define a question. Identify the most problematic issue you have found in using the six types of overtness about task. Frame it as a question to which you need an answer (e.g., "What are my responsibilities on this project?" "Why am I still here?" "How do I know if I'm making progress?"). Be as specific as possible.

3. Define your approach. First, consider "who": identify someone with whom an objective discussion of this question might produce useful results. Then think about "what": consider conversation starters that open with a statement of your understanding rather than a question that will put the other person on the defensive. Finally, determine "how": decide how quick or thorough your conversation will be and how much focus you will place on issues of task versus people.

4. Define your need for agreement: Decide what agreement, if any, you need from the other person. Be prepared to agree to disagree about other things to avoid losing sight of the original topic of your discussion.

5. Have the actual conversation, and make it as productive as possible. See what you learn, thank the person for his or her time, and then decide whether the answers you obtained are sufficient or if you should repeat the cycle with the same person or some-

one else. *Or* you may have an imaginary conversation. In your mind's eye, visualize yourself and the other person having the interaction that begins with the starter you've defined. Carefully walk through the scenario, including your statements and the other person's response. In some cases, you can gain useful ideas and insights without even involving another person.

PART 2

GROWING YOUR CRYSTAL

Example is not the main thing in influencing others.
It is the only thing.

—ALBERT SCHWEITZER

4 Beginning Your Crystal

One reason organizational culture change is such a compelling notion is because of the sheer scale involved. Change a company's location, business processes, or even product line, and you only change aspects of how it does business. But change its culture, and you've changed everything about what it's trying to be and do in the world and what it's like to work within it. When a culture change happens, changes to things like business process and product line flow naturally; everything ultimately aligns to fit the new culture.

That's the ideal, anyway, and it can happen. But in what time frame? Most of us tend to think in terms of quick, noticeable changes: the quarterly report mentality. When you're changing a new product line or office location, you can imagine or perceive what's different. Culture change, on the other hand, is not implemented immediately; it develops slowly because it is a natural, organic process. Attempts to "manage" natural processes without respect for their inherent timelines tend to fall flat. You can no more mandate a change in your workplace culture than you can the growth rate of a plant. Wanting things to go faster may be very human, but using Gantt charts, developing project plans, and exerting time pressure won't make your oak tree grow more quickly.

If there is a way to speed up a natural process, it involves focusing on how the process works and what it requires. In the case of a plant, you must not only sow the right seed, but you must find a location with the right soil, water, and climatic conditions. In the case of a cultural crystal, you must start with a seed crystal and then encourage the growth of the crystal by helping neighboring particles—in this case, people—to "attach."

Culture of Two

Consider again the crystalline network of your workplace. Figure 4.1 is familiar, except that it indicates a new attachment between you and one of your coworkers. You and that coworker have a "network upgrade," an enhanced link between you. You're both being fully overt about your tasks and seeking clarity in your interactions with each other. As a result, you experience better information transfer and find it easier to support each other's work. That's not to say you never have disagreements, but on the whole, your interactions are focused and the results tend to be positive.

If you're lucky, you might already have at least one relationship like this, someone with whom you interact productively, get along well, and share mutual support. As you read about overtness and clarity, you may have thought about that person, realizing that you were reading about things the two of you had already learned to do when working together.

FIGURE 4.1 A single-link upgrade

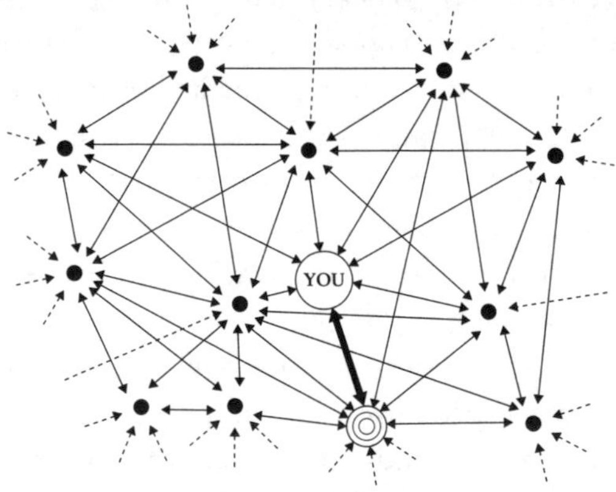

Notice that this doesn't necessarily imply that you're friends on a personal level. You may or may not spend time together outside of work, share the same social values or family situations, or agree on issues such as politics or religion. Indeed, you may never have even broached some of those topics. What's pertinent is that the two of you are overt with each other about what you need to do and seek clarity about appropriate topics and goals whenever you communicate. This leads to mutual respect and trust. Your relationship helps both of you get your work done, and it might even make the work a little more fun.

If you don't have such a relationship, don't despair. Your first task in building the culture around you is to find one. That's all, just one. Remember, culture change is all about using your *choice* about what patterns you will demonstrate as a *force* to influence and inspire change. You start demonstrating here and now on a limited and manageable basis by role-modeling new patterns to one person, someone who you would like to be the first to attach to your new cultural crystal.

Why not start with more than one? Why not two, five, or nine? After all, you're already demonstrating to everyone all the time anyway. Why not target a whole group of people for your first additions? The problem is that when you begin to multiply five people by six types of overtness and three types of clarity, your project can quickly become overwhelming, and you may give up or make major mistakes. Your nascent patterns of behavior are new and fragile at this point; treat your new crystal with care. You can certainly talk about this book and the ideas it contains with whomever you like, and other people may certainly observe your demonstrations; but for the moment, limit your first crystal addition to one person.

Who should you choose? You can pick anyone with whom you work on a regular basis: coworker, manager, employee, or customer. This is not the time to choose the most troublesome person in your work life! Aim at the easiest target first. Choose someone you really like, someone with whom you already have some trust and a positive history and are most likely to have success. Write the person's name in your notebook—in ink!

Is This Networking?

Much has been written about the importance of professional networking, and supportive human networks are critical in a variety of circumstances. Whether you require a piece of important information, a lead on a new job, or the name of a good potential employee, your professional network is where you look.

Culture building is complementary to effective networking, but it is not the same thing. In traditional networking, the goal is to make contact with someone who might be "good to know," establish a relationship, and then keep an active connection should either of you be able to help the other in the future. You reach far from your established circle—past the limits of Figure 4.1—and build connections in new areas. Then, through conversations geared toward mutual benefit, you and your new contact explore how you might link your two crystalline structures, now or in the future, by learning about each others' work and helping each other. In networking, you begin with someone who is metaphorically distant, and then build a bridge of mutual benefit back to where you are.

Crystal building, on the other hand, starts locally. You choose someone you know well and work with most often. You enhance that communication link first, with an eye toward building outward from there. The end goal is the same: to create a growing list of trusted contacts. But in crystal building, the first thing you add is trust, not contacts. You're not reaching past the limits of Figure 4.1. You're working within it, improving and changing your relationships with those around you one at a time, until you have re-created the patterns of work that all of you together use to do your jobs. That's why the first person you select should be someone with whom you already work closely.

Teach by Example and Only by Example

How exactly are you supposed to encourage that chosen colleague to adopt your new patterns of workplace behavior? How do you get someone else to start practicing overtness about tasks and clarity within relationships? The answer to this question will depend on specifics about the person and your relationship. But there is one aspect of adult education that will serve you well in your new role as culture teacher no matter what: the power of role-modeling.

Role-modeling, in its most basic form, means that you must do what you're suggesting the other person do. Ralph Waldo Emerson said, "What you do speaks so loudly that I cannot hear what you say." This is common sense, yet we have all observed someone saying one thing and doing another. At best, such people come across as confused; more often, they seem disingenuous and untrustworthy. This is too important a point to overlook; it's the reason this book started with y-o-u. If you're going to try to get someone else to practice overtness about task and clarity within relationships, you'd better be practicing both of them yourself!

In fact, teaching by demonstration is the only effective way to influence other adults in your workplace. Any other approach will fail. The moment you present yourself to coworkers as "the professor of the new culture," your credibility and influence will evaporate. Classroom-style instruction may work well in some circumstances, but it's not the right approach when it comes to changing culture. The strategy that will work for you—the only strategy—is for you to become that which you wish to encourage and then let others learn from your example. As Mohandas Gandhi said, "We must be the change we wish to see."

Begin with Purpose and Clarity

As always, overtness about your workplace purpose is a great place to start. Hopefully, you've penned a tentative version of your summary outputs list. (This list is always subject to revision.) If your list is well written, it should easily lend itself to being shared verbally. In fact, as your cultural crystal grows, you will be verbalizing your summary outputs frequently and listening for feedback from a wide array of people.

Note that *listening* for feedback does not necessarily imply *asking* for it. In some cases, it may be appropriate to ask someone for his or her thoughts about your summary outputs list. More often, however, it is preferable to simply recite your "current understanding subject to change" and let the other person decide what to discuss next. This strategy will help you to get a manageable amount of spontaneous, high-quality feedback rather than a voluminous amount of forced, low-quality feedback.

In any case, feedback is not your primary goal at the moment. Your real intent is to encourage the other person to think and talk about his or her own workplace purpose. Obviously, the more trusting your relationship with that person, the easier this will be. The organizational relationship between you also comes into play, a topic we'll address later in this chapter.

Remember that, no matter what, preparation is your ally. Before you attempt your conversation, prepare using the three definitions that go along with seeking clarity:

1. Define your question. In this case, the question you're trying to answer has two parts: (a) How can you best share your workplace purpose? and (b) what is the other person's purpose? Your only goal is information exchange.

2. Define your approach. As always, be prepared to interact with the other person in ways that maximize his or her comfort, matching your pace and focus. For example, if she's someone who likes to study everything in writing, be sure to bring along a printed copy of your summary outputs list.

3. Define your need for agreement. In this case, your aim is shared understanding, not agreement. You can't expect a utopia in which everyone agrees with you, nor do you require one. Begin with the desire for information exchange alone; issues of agreement that demand resolution will surface soon enough.

Notice that in trying to role-model being overt, you have immediately become a role model for seeking clarity too. Task and relationship, as always, are intertwined. The desire to share workplace purpose leads to the need to define your question, approach, and need for agreement. The use of those clear definitions in your interaction with the person you've chosen creates a smoother conversation and improves the flow of information.

Beyond Purpose

The reason for starting with workplace purpose is that it naturally leads to the other five types of overtness: impact, incentive, progress, resources, and capability. The question of where your conversation goes next is open-ended. It's easy to imagine, for example, a discussion about purpose leading to a conversation about resources. What you're trying to accomplish and what you need to get there are closely related topics. Yet the discussion could just as easily turn elsewhere, such as to incentive ("why I'm excited to be doing this") or capability ("what I need to learn").

To attempt to script an entire conversation in advance would be unnecessary—and a mistake. You already have the relationship, the ideas about what to discuss, and the knowledge of how your colleague will respond. If you start with a trusted person and begin with an honest sharing of workplace purpose, the rest will emerge naturally.

How you can best help it to emerge, however, may depend in part on the organizational relationship between you and your colleague.

If You Are the Manager

As a manager or leader, you are a constant role model to your direct (and indirect) reports, whether you like it or not. In that regard, the people in your organization may be the easiest to add to your cultural crystal. You have a lot of say regarding how they do things and a lot of visibility into what they do. Plus, because nearly everyone is a manager-watcher, your demonstration by example holds more weight with employees than with peers or managers. Formal authority can be a good thing. When trust is high, some managers have great success beginning their cultural crystal within their own employee base.

Remember, though, that the blade of your clout cuts both ways. Constant attention from employees means constant scrutiny. If you say one thing and do another, they'll know it. Whether aloud or privately, they'll call you on it, and your credibility will be lost. Your risk of appearing hypocritical is highest when you suggest that an employee try a new, more effective pattern of working: make sure you consistently role-model what you request.

Overtness About Purpose if You Are the Manager

When you begin with overtness about purpose, remember that your role as a manager carries implications. Resist the temptation to start by asking for the employee's purpose first; an innocent question like "Can you summarize what you're doing?" can be very intimidating when posed by a manager! Your employee may wonder if you're unhappy with his or her work or may even start to worry about job security ("Why does my manager suddenly want a summary statement of my work? What is she going to do with it?"). Instead, start the conversation by sharing your own summary outputs list. "This is a statement of my output priorities," you might say, as you hand a written copy to your employee. "Which of them would you like to discuss as being most closely related to your work?" By indicating that you're trying to build a fuller understanding of your purpose and how his or her work fits into it, you set the stage for mutual understanding and avoid initiating an "inquisition" that might lead to more posturing than information exchange. As the conversation continues, try to initiate dialogue about editing your own list, teaching by example that such editing is acceptable and valuable.

Overtness About Impact if You Are the Manager

Addressing overtness about both past and future instances of impact with a staff member can be particularly powerful. If the impact was in the past, you have the opportunity to reinforce the benefits that he or she has produced. Encourage frequently; celebrate often! Do so as soon as possible after your employee does something well, and be as specific as you can about the impact, why it is important, and what your direct report did right. Avoid mixing positive and negative feedback—allow a whole conversation to be about what was done well.[1] If the impact is planned for the future, you can paint a picture of why your employee's work is so important. If you can help him or her connect impact with incentive—how the results of the work will produce value for both the company and the employee—you'll have an even easier time holding useful conversations about this type of overtness.

Overtness About Incentives if You Are the Manager

Conversations involving overtness about incentive can be tricky. Like anyone, your employee would prefer a job that is engaging and exciting. On the other hand, he or she wants to be seen as a willing worker and a team player. The idea of talking with you, the manager, about why he or she "likes this job" can be unsettling; the idea of discussing what he or she wishes were different can be downright unpleasant. Be cognizant of this difficulty. Try to open the door for conversation about what work your employee finds most satisfying without initiating a complaint session that leaves both of you frustrated. Frame the conversation as a search for information you want for the future. Explain that you would like to know more about your employee's favorite parts of the job, so that over time you can provide more of those opportunities. Seed the conversation with positive observations: "You seem to have a talent for interacting with customers on the phone. Is that something you enjoy?" Be positive about possibilities, but be honest about reality. Don't promise anything you can't deliver.

Overtness About Progress if You Are the Manager

Discussing overtness about progress and the visibility system an employee uses to track his or her individual progress can be difficult too. Because you're the manager, when all goes well, you shouldn't see your employees' visibility systems—only their results. You wouldn't look over a person's to-do list, for example, unless you perceived a problem with his output. You certainly wouldn't want your own supervisor micromanaging you this way, so be careful not to become a micromanager yourself. Instead, try to learn about visibility systems in safe ways. Congratulate successful employees on their performance and ask about how they track their progress. Avoid asking them to do anything differently—as in, "While you're making that checklist, you could easily e-mail it to me"—or they'll become reluctant to share. Be clear that your only goal is to learn something that you might someday share with someone else, perhaps saying, "I don't want you to do anything differently, I'd just like to learn what makes you so successful in case I need to coach someone else in the future." In framing your discussion this way, you'll reinforce the importance of visibility systems and prepare yourself to deal with other employees about how they might become self-reliant by improving their own systems.

Overtness About Resources if You Are the Manager

If the conversation turns to overtness about resources, remember that such conversations often begin with something the employee lacks. Trying to produce output in the absence of needed resources can be a frustrating, demoralizing experience; different employees will handle it differently. Some may become agitated and approach you with the basic orientation that you, as their manager, "had better get this resolved." Others may internalize the lack of resources as their own failure and be quick to blame themselves—or be reluctant to raise the issue at all. But whether your employee is pointing the finger at you or himself, your challenge as manager is to steer the conversation toward the output required, the specific resource needed, and how the two of you together might obtain it. Don't fall into the trap of blaming anyone for the "lack." Focus instead on solutions: "What additional resources would you need to deliver your outputs?" Remember too that there may be an iterative effect here: if the acquisition of a needed resource is complex or difficult enough, getting that resource may become a project in itself and appear as a new item on someone's summary outputs list.

Overtness About Capability if You Are the Manager

Discussing overtness about capability with an employee can be easy or difficult. Much depends on the level of trust between you and on how you frame the discussion. Are you talking about a gap in your

Quick Video: Encouraging Excellent Performance

Visit www.MakeWorkGreat.com for a short video segment about how to encourage someone to replicate a positive behavior. This is also an easy bit of information to share if you're trying to describe the contents of this chapter to a trusted friend or colleague.

employee's skills, saying that he or she is missing a necessary ability? Or are you discussing a growth area—a way in which the employee can learn something new and become more valuable in the future? There's no guarantee of success with either conversation, but you're less likely to inspire defensive behavior if you can stay focused on the future. Be careful not to accidentally suggest a gap where there isn't one. On the other hand, if you must address a legitimate gap, clearly identify the current state of performance and the change in ability or skills required; limit the conversation to a specific skill or topic. It's best to have such conversations just before the employee can use them rather than just after he or she has made a mistake![2]

If You Are the Employee

If you have decided to add your own manager to your new crystal, your approach must be different than the one described in the previous section. Many people feel that, as the employee, they're obligated to do what their manager says and not question or disrupt the status quo. The utility of this "blind obedience" approach to employment is debatable, especially in the (frequent) cases where employees have some piece of knowledge or expertise the manager lacks. But even setting that debate aside, an obligation to follow directives does not translate to an obligation to follow outmoded patterns of information transfer. Those who become talented at influencing managers and leaders above them in their organizational hierarchies frequently report that "managing their manager" is tremendously important to their output and satisfaction at work.

Quick Video: Changing Behavior

Visit www.MakeWorkGreat.com for a short video segment about how to advise someone regarding a gap in skills or performance. This is also an easy bit of information to share if you're trying to describe the contents of this chapter to a trusted friend or colleague.

Role-modeling is still your best bet. When it comes to influencing your manager, nothing is more powerful than allowing him or her to see how you do your work and the fact that you're producing results. The better you are as an employee, the better you can be as a role model to those above you in your organization's hierarchy. The key is to demonstrate a specific type of overtness effectively in a short amount of time. That way, there's no sense that you're talking out of turn or being disrespectful of anyone's authority.

Overtness About Purpose if You Are the Employee

At the beginning, you may not feel comfortable asking your manager to verbalize his or her workplace purpose, but you can use your own summary outputs list to open each of your interactions: "I just want to take a few moments to ensure that I'm still focused on the correct priorities, so here's how I see my job." This way, you open the door for useful conversation and demonstrate your commitment to the job, all in under two minutes. At the same time, you pave the way for a future conversation about your manager's overall workplace purpose, which may ultimately be an inspiration to develop and share his or her own summary outputs list.

Overtness About Impact if You Are the Employee

Impact should be one of the easiest things to talk about with your manager. Whether you're bringing up a brief synopsis of something you've already accomplished or asking the specific value of a new piece of work you've been assigned, be sure to share the credit for the impact you're discussing. For example, "I got some feedback from accounting that the new processes you asked me to develop are saving about three hours per week. I thought you'd be as proud of that as I am." Or for a new piece of work, "It's clear to me that when I finish this, it will increase the number of high-revenue products we can offer. Do you have any other view of what this will accomplish from a broader perspective?" Be inclusive, impact-focused, and quick. Allow your manager to make the decision about whether to delve more deeply or move on.

Overtness About Incentives if You Are the Employee

When talking with your manager about your incentives, keep your initial conversations positive. Avoid leading with what you don't like about your work. Find positives: "I really enjoy one particular aspect of this work," you might say. "That's the chance to research new approaches to old problems." Be as specific as you can, and show gratitude: "I want to thank you for this opportunity and let you know it's something I like in case similar opportunities arise." In less than a minute you have role-modeled overtness about your own incentives without doing anything that remotely resembles complaining.

Overtness About Progress if You Are the Employee

Sharing how you track your progress can be tricky. Your obligation under normal circumstances is to inform your manager regarding the current status of your output requirements. Going deeper—to the level of the visibility systems you use to track that status—runs the risk of inviting unnecessary scrutiny or micromanagement. As with each type of overtness, only you can decide if and when it's appropriate to have this conversation. When you do, try to find a way to let your manager know you have a system for keeping track of your work without initially going into too much detail about how it works. An offer to share your system directly with colleagues might be a good strategy. Or you could disclose just part of the system—"By the way, I post my daily checklist of tasks on the wall in my work area to help myself stay on track." Keep your intention well defined. You want to spend a minute or two role-modeling the value of visibility systems, but you're not trying to convince your manager to implement your system on a widespread basis or to use it as a way to influence his or her opinion of you.

Overtness About Resources if You Are the Employee

You probably already discuss questions of resources with your manager. When you don't have something you need to do your job and you're not able to get it at your own level, your only choice is to escalate. To role-model resource-based conversations even more effectively, all you have to do is occasionally interject a comment about resources for one of your summary outputs when you don't have a problem: "In accomplishing this, I'll make use of the following resources [list them]. I don't see any issue in acquiring those resources at this point, but I'll naturally let you know if any problems come up." A statement like this role-models overtness about resources in less than 60 seconds.

Overtness About Capability if You Are the Employee

Many people get nervous about discussing capability with superiors. Some feel uncomfortable about articulating their own strengths; others are especially hesitant to disclose their weaknesses. Even when trust is high between you and your manager, this can be a daunting conversation. But consider this—sooner or later, most managers are going to be required to give you feedback on your strengths and weaknesses. While you don't want to boast, and you certainly don't wish to provide ammunition against yourself, it may be in your best interest to help your manager develop that feedback. Seek ways to be succinctly overt about your capability: "I'm proud of the skills I've developed in this [give specific] area, and would appreciate your feedback so I can get even better." Or, "I feel like I have a lot to learn about [specific area], and I thought you might be able to help me." By initiating the conversation, you have much more control over its scope and direction than if you wait for the feedback to "happen to you." And by disclosing your needs in advance, you reduce the potential for your manager to complain about you. Instead, you initiate a conversation about how to work together to obtain a needed element for your output.

If You Are a Peer

We have just addressed in some detail how you might role-model overtness and clarity to either an employee or a superior. What if you have decided to begin your crystal by adding a peer?

The problem with the word *peer* is that it can mean many different things. Anyone with whom you have neither a formal reporting relationship nor an obvious difference in organizational hierarchy is usually considered a peer. Your "peer" could direct your work, have his or her work directed by you, or do tasks only peripherally related to yours. Depending on your definition, he or she could even be a customer, supplier, or member of an entirely different company.

Obviously, elements of the approaches for employees and managers apply here. The more you direct this person's work, the closer your approach will be to that described in "If You Are the Manager." The more the other person directs your work, the closer your approach will be to the one in "If You Are the Employee."

But there is one other thing to consider. Role-modeling, particularly with peers, can be enhanced with a moderate amount of explanation or narration. Demonstrating a skill or approach is one thing; bringing it to the level of consciousness by explaining what you're doing creates even more opportunities for learning.

Imagine, for example, a conversation in which you are seeking clarity by defining the need for agreement. You might already be inclined to ask a question such as, "Could we agree to disagree regarding methodology and focus instead on defining a mutually acceptable output requirement?" In role-modeling to a peer, you might add one more sentence: "Personally, I find that limiting the need for agreement in advance like this saves time by keeping the conversation on topic." The few extra seconds of narration brings what you're doing to the level of consciousness. Just be sure to make it a personal statement rather than a didactic one. You're not the teacher, and you're not trying to direct the other person's activity. You are simply giving him or her an opportunity to recognize what you are doing already.

When role-modeling like this, your natural inclination may be to hide your mistakes. But you're bound to make missteps, and in fact, they're helpful. When it comes to role-modeling with peers, the key to errors is to highlight them. For example, if you're suggesting that a coworker create a verbalized summary outputs list, you might begin by sharing your own. In reviewing what you've written, he or she may point out an incorrect assumption about required output. You may be tempted to gloss over that specific issue or to stop and discuss it on the spot. From a culture-demonstrating perspective, however, your best approach is first to acknowledge it and then to incorporate it into the broader learning experience: "As you can see, I'm still learning too, and you've given me something to think about." In approaching your error this way, you demonstrate humility, you maintain the learning environment for both of you, and you subtly remind the other person to learn from his or her own future mistakes too.

Your goal is always to demonstrate new patterns without coming across as a know-it-all. By consistently demonstrating your own overtness about tasks and clarity within relationships, and by describing both your successes and errors in a balanced way, you give the other person more opportunities to internalize those new patterns of behavior for themselves.

Be Careful of What You Role-Model

As we close this chapter, one final, critical message is worth considering: be very careful about what patterns you demonstrate. As a role model—especially if you're a leader or manager—everything you do is in the spotlight.

One of my most painful experiences of this phenomenon happened in a day-long simulation training I was running. The simulation has been refined over the years to mimic the complex, multivariate, early information age workplace that is the topic of this book. Participants work in teams on a complex matrix of tasks—practicing team building, improving their crystalline network, and learning from experience and from each other how best to approach their work successfully and not burn out. Feedback is consistently positive; people quickly see the links between the challenges of the simulation and the chaos they face in their own jobs, and they're elated to learn that the chaos can be managed and successful outputs achieved without a 90-hour workweek.

This particular group was divided into two teams of roughly a dozen people each. Each team worked within its own version of the simulated workplace. They started with the same boundary conditions and constraints, the same leadership structure (a team leader with a small group of directors overseeing everyone else), and the same output requirements.

The disparity between the teams was noticeable within the first hour, and it grew all day. One had conflict; the other had output. One worked smoothly and quietly and produced a record result; the other was rife with disagreement and failed to meet even the most basic output standard. At the end of the day, the struggling team's members berated me, the session, and its goals, while the participants from the successful team beamed with the notion that their work was about to get better and thanked me profusely for their newfound insights. As an instructor, it was a surreal experience: two groups, 10 feet apart in the same room, giving feedback about what sounded like two entirely different sessions.

What was so different about the teams? It wasn't membership. Everyone in the session worked together regularly in the same organization; they all knew each other already and tended to get along. The two "teams" were simply the result of a random division of the group; I knew of no difference between them in overall intelligence, capability, or job descriptions. I had also discussed the group's current state and needs with its leader, and we had agreed the training was appropriate for everyone. In fact, I had conducted the same training with other members of the group before (and since) and encountered no similar problems.

What happened? In preparing the two team leaders for their day's assignment, I missed a critical detail. As it turned out, the leader of the team that would ultimately struggle—who was a highly capable worker in his own sphere—had a strong belief that any workplace simulation was less important than the pile of work waiting back at his office. He didn't mention this specifically, and I didn't ask about it. Like a good CEO, I focused on what I wanted him to produce and what he had at his disposal. Like a good leader, he interacted with me about the topic at hand, learned what he could, and agreed to try his best. I strongly believe, by the way, that he did try his best. I saw no evidence to suggest that he purposely caused any of the difficulty that ensued on his team.

Yet he did cause it—right from the start. By interviewing the other team members and reflecting on what I observed, I learned what had happened. It began with the leader in the first 20 minutes of the session. The first time I asked the teams to meet independently and begin planning, he laid the foundation for his team's downfall.

How? His high level of distraction came through in everything he did. In subtle ways, he communicated to his second-tier managers that "whatever you do is fine; it doesn't really matter." At that moment, when he was supposed to be explaining to his group what they had to do, he instead essentially told them, "Figure it out if you want to—or not." This leader unwittingly positioned himself as the exact opposite of Emma (my supervisor from Chapter 1); he was distracted, disengaged, and disinterested. And his team heard his message loud and clear. "Figure it out if you want to—or not" became their operational philosophy for the day.

The detriment of this cultural pattern was widespread. In one of many examples, an individual tasked with overseeing quality of production highlighted some mistakes in plenty of time to correct them. The people doing the work were overwrought with conflict among themselves and basically told the quality control person to keep quiet. She responded with, "Fine, you'll see," and walked away. The leader watched indifferently, and the other team members saw his indifference.

With perfect hindsight, I can think of a few interventions that might have saved the situation. Certainly, finding a different leader would have helped. But a new start—either at the outset of the activity or anywhere along the way—could also have worked with the same leader. Firing isn't always the answer. What if the leader had stopped everything, owned up to his role in the problems at hand, and asked everyone to regroup with the notion of finding answers to their most pressing questions? Had the leader changed what he was role-modeling at any point in the process, I believe the results would have been quite different.

Actually, any team member could have done the same thing. In my haste to help the leader "on the fly," I failed to encourage the rest of the participants to produce their own cultural crystal. I now realize my limited intervention time would have been better spent coaching the other team members to role-model their own environment. One or two people could have stood up, asked for a pause, and suggested that the group get more specific about the relationship between activity and outcome. I've seen this happen in other teams with positive results, initiating complete turnarounds in output and stress level despite a few problems "from above." A cultural crystal can start anywhere.

You are the role model. Whoever you are, be careful what you're teaching by example. Also, keep a watchful eye on what appears in the culture around you. That, after all, is the mirror that shows you what you're creating. Be sure that what you're making is, in fact, great.

EXERCISES

1. Select the first person you wish to add to your cultural crystal: a trusted employee, manager, or peer with whom you already have a positive and productive relationship.

---

2. Plan to have a conversation with that person about workplace purpose—yours and his or hers—and see where the conversation leads in terms of the other areas of overtness. Be sure to define your question, your approach, and your need for agreement in advance. Also, review the section of this chapter that matches the organizational relationship between you (employee, manager, or peer).

---

3. Have the interaction, note what goes well and what doesn't, and make plans for the next conversation.

---

5 Organic Growth

Here we are, halfway through. Hopefully, you're getting the idea that although this type of culture change may not be easy, it is relatively simple. All you have to do is follow two steps:

1. Decide to decide—and decide! That is, decide to be someone who sets cultural precedents at least as often as you follow them. Then decide what precedents you will set.

2. Gain support. Encourage some of the people around you to follow your new precedents and to pass them along to others.

You have already defined your new precedents and "attached" the first new member of your crystal. Now it's time to think a little bigger and consider who else you might enlist. During this process, we'll get more specific about the meaning of "adding a member to your crystal" and why, from another person's perspective, he or she would want to "join" your group.

Rinse and Repeat?

You've selected the person with whom you have the most influence and begun to role-model overtness about task and clarity within relationships. Now, all you have to do is repeat the process with everyone else, right?

Yes and no. You'll certainly want others to join your crystal. But the idea of repeating Chapter 4 over and over again, trying to "sell" everyone around you on the idea of becoming part of your crystal, should make you nervous. For one thing, you don't want to spend your days as a culture salesperson. For another, no matter who you are, there are people in your workplace who will be oblivious, unreceptive, or even hostile to your attempts to role-model any new patterns or precedents. Certainly, you should practice overtness and clarity with them as best you can. But trying to use the tools from Chapter 4 to produce changes in their behavior is setting yourself up for failure and frustration.

The good news is that you don't have to. Allowing the willing ones to attach themselves to your crystal is enough.

Multiplication of Influence

As soon as you add the first person to your crystal, your part of the pond begins to freeze. You're no longer a culture of only one. Instead, you're using the multiplicative effect of the crystalline network to your advantage. You're broadcasting your new precedents to an expanding audience, and your influence on the cultural patterns around you will grow accordingly.

Consider your potential reach—the number of people to whom you can role-model—when you're working alone. Your ability to demonstrate new patterns of interaction is limited to those with whom you have direct links. And let's face it, some of those people will be more receptive than others. Instead of worrying about the difficult ones, Chapter 4 asked you to focus on the easiest one and to add him or her as the first new member of your cultural crystal. Figure 5.1 shows the initial scope of your direct influence, along with your first addition.

When you consider the size of your overall organization, this might not look too promising. But remember that your first addition has

FIGURE 5.1 The limits of your potential reach when you role-model alone

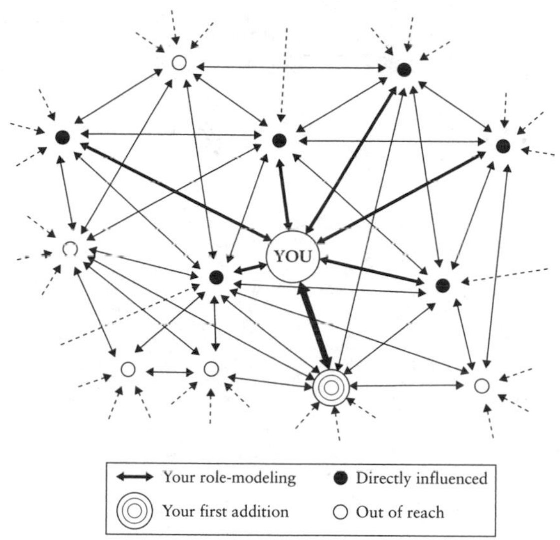

his or her own network of contacts. By adding a person, you are indirectly connected to others via his or her links. Actually, your first addition exposes others in the network to your new cultural patterns in three different ways, as shown in Figure 5.2.

First, consider the colleagues with whom you don't work on a regular basis. They may influence your workplace, but you can't role-model directly because you don't have enough interaction with them. You don't have a direct link, but your new partner-in-culture might! He or she can influence some of the people you can't, demonstrating new cultural patterns to those you couldn't reach.

Second, consider those to whom both you and your new partner-in-culture are connected. With both of you role-modeling overtness and clarity, those people will get two different examples of how your new precedents work. Think of the power of this strategy: what they see you doing, they also see someone else doing. It's like having mul-

FIGURE 5.2 The multiplication of your potential reach by adding another person to your crystal

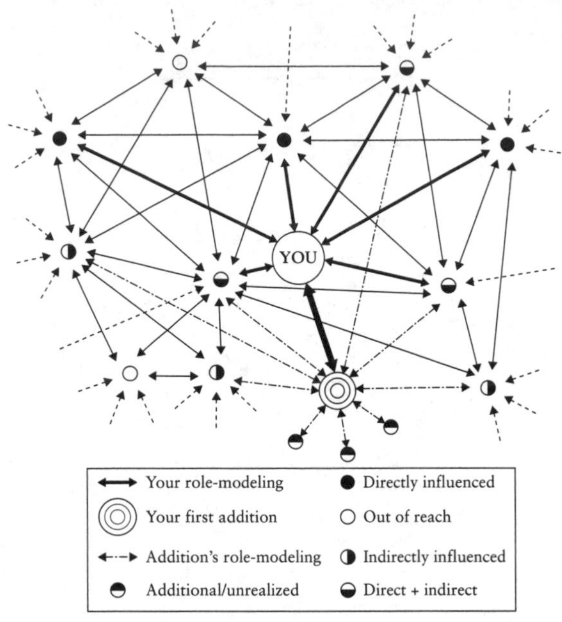

tiple people independently recommend the same product; the credibility of the recommendation skyrockets.

Finally, remember that you only perceive a part of the overall crystalline network of your workplace. Those dotted lines that extend off the page are the people who aren't a part of your daily work life but do exert influence within their own spheres. If your new partner-in-culture is connected to some of these people, the effects of your influence will go there too. Like a ripple in a giant lake, the changes you're role-modeling radiate beyond the limits of your awareness.

In Figure 5.2, enrolling a single person in your new patterns of behavior means that your new cultural patterns gain indirect influence over three people (◑), direct and indirect influence over three people (◒), and unrealized influence over three additional people

(◓). Obviously, your own network of contacts will look different, and it may or may not be worthwhile to try to draw it. What is important is to understand the dynamics of the system at play and to remember that quality trumps quantity when it comes to adding a new member to your crystal. Role-model consistently to everyone, but spend the bulk of your culture-demonstrating efforts on a small number of additions with whom you have a high likelihood of success. Take a lesson from leaders such as Gandhi and Mother Teresa, who built up amazing amounts of influence from positive individual connections, and use the multiplicative effect to your advantage.

Success Equals . . . ?

Let's pause for a moment. In the spirit of overtness about purpose, we need to be precise about what it means to have a successful addition to your cultural crystal. You can say that you have fully enrolled another person in your cultural crystal when the following are true:

- You're able to interact regarding the six types of overtness (purpose, impact, incentive, progress, resources, and capability) with regard to your work and that person's.
- Your interactions are built on a foundation of clarity (with a well-defined question, correct approach, and defined need for agreement).
- Through your interactions, you have built a mutual understanding of each other's roles, challenges, and constraints.
- You both characterize your relationship as mutually beneficial.
- You see evidence that he or she practices and role-models overtness about task and clarity within relationships with others.

Notice the strictness of these criteria. If you're serious about creating change, you need to be serious about recognizing the change, even if it comes slowly, just one or two people at a time. By defining an addition to your crystal using these conditions, you draw a distinction between someone who is in the process of being added and someone who is already a member.

Reflect briefly upon this important distinction. If culture is nothing but the aggregate default behavior of everyone around you, changing culture means changing behavior. The change must propagate throughout the system. You don't need to force this proliferation, but it's absolutely necessary that you recognize the extent to which the new patterns have spread. The difference between someone in the process of being added and someone who has already been added is the difference between a planted seed and a sapling.

Because you're broadcasting a new set of patterns and watching to see who is willing to incorporate them, there's a loose analogy to sales here. Consider the funnel-shaped model in Figure 5.3, which represents the different populations of people in your environment and their relationship to your new cultural crystal. Similar figures are often drawn to represent prospective buyers: in both cases, the process begins at the top with the widest population and narrows down, step by step, to the critical few. In sales, prospects become leads, leads become opportunities, and opportunities become transactions.

Of course, you won't be a salesperson; your "product"—your bundle of new cultural precedents—will either sell itself or not. Your job is simply to pay attention to who is "buying" and where those people are in the process of adoption. In that sense, you are more of a market analyst. First you recognize candidates from everyone around you, then some candidates become additions in progress, and ultimately some of those additions in progress become new members. Even if it takes a whole year, the addition of just a few new members to your crystal can make a tremendous impact in the broader culture of your environment. If you want to prove this to yourself, try redrawing the network of Figure 5.2 with the addition of a second partner in culture for you and an additional partner in culture for one of your two new partners. Start with a big sheet of paper, because you will need to expand the figure substantially to capture all of the new layers of influence.

FIGURE 5.3 The funnel model of workplace populations and their relationship to your crystal

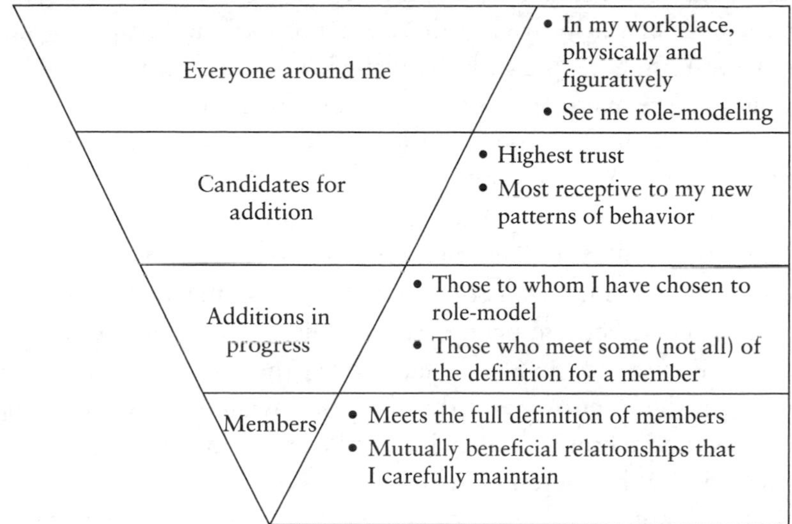

As you practice the new behaviors of overtness and clarity yourself and role-model them to people around you, you're showcasing your new precedents. It will be apparent from their responses which of these possible candidates are receptive to the changes you're demonstrating—in other words, the ones who will "tune in" to your broadcast. If you don't already share a high level of trust with them, it will begin to develop as they become your best candidates for addition. When you have satisfied yourself that you're ready to spend some time and energy trying to work on a second addition, these receptive individuals are the pool from which you can select one.

There's even more good news. If you're role-modeling consistently, your second and subsequent additions will be easier than your first. Not only will you already know who your candidates are, but your previous display of new precedents will have laid the groundwork to help them convert themselves from candidates to additions in progress more quickly.

Potential Additions

The use of the word *candidate* is no accident. In the same way that you would screen candidates for a job, you should be screening others for inclusion in your crystal. You're not looking for just anyone; you want to find people with the inclination and ability to make the changes you're making. Be on the lookout for superstars!

As the influence of your broadcast begins to snowball, you may find yourself with more candidates than you expect. Ultimately, people will come to you and essentially ask to be part of your crystal, because they will be influenced by the network around them and see the benefit of joining (something we'll discuss later in this chapter). This may be difficult to believe early in the process, but consider the math in Figure 5.2. Sooner or later, even the most resistant people will be in the minority, and through the invisible forces of change described in the Prologue, they'll be pulled toward your new patterns of behavior without even realizing it.

But let's not get ahead of ourselves. For now, while your crystal is in its early growth stage, you'll need to pay conscious attention to your broadcast. Our definition of a successful addition is strict; it's far better to succeed with a few than to fail with many. So let's consider the obvious—and not-so-obvious—groups that might be early candidates to receive your broadcast.

Broadcast to Your Organization

If you're a manager, you probably already considered choosing your first member from among your direct reports. Now consider the benefits of adding an entire group of employees to your crystal. Whether you're in a direct management role or a project or team leadership role, you exert influence over the people in your charge. One of the benefits of crystal building with these people is that you can incorporate the new norms for behavior into group settings as well as individual ones, making your role-modeling more efficient. Imagine a portion of a team meeting in which each member presents his or her summary outputs list. Or a column on your staff meeting agenda that defines the need for agreement for each item of discussion. If your employees interact with each other regularly, or if they have employees of their own, the multiplicative effect of your crystalline network could work very quickly.

Good managers and leaders often create a positive subculture within their groups. Doing so consciously may be a great mutual benefit proposition, a way to increase your group's output and enjoyment while also growing your cultural crystal.

As you add employees, however, remember that their frequent interaction means they're comparing notes about you! Your responsibility is to treat them fairly and equitably. Equitable treatment doesn't mean identical treatment; there's nothing wrong with helping different employees develop different skills or developing a mentorship relationship with one person. But *equitable* does mean equal. Take care to avoid anything remotely resembling favoritism. Stay fully within both the letter and the spirit of fairness, as defined by your company's policies and your own ethics. To infuse even the slightest bit of anything else into your new culture, even accidentally, would be counter to your intent and act like salt to your emerging ice crystal.

Broadcast to Your Role Set

You needn't limit your thinking to those who report to you. Another group to consider early in the process is your primary role set. Recall from the Prologue that this small group of people—typically between five and eight—exerts the most influence over what you do at work. You already have a lot of interaction with the members of your role set; they are often on the receiving end of your output. As a result, you have many opportunities to interact with them, role-model to them, and—if they're receptive—encourage them to become part of your new cultural crystal.

Your manager is most likely one of these people. Whoever the rest of them are (employees, customers, colleagues, managers, or executives), you have an opportunity to showcase your new patterns of behavior in the context of delivering what they already ask of you.

If you're unsure how to broadcast to this group, consider a simple model for growing the network between you and your role set by creating a crystal of ICE (identify, connect, explain):

1. Identify the five to eight people who comprise your primary role set and list them in your notebook.

2. Connect with each of them. Whether it's a greeting in the parking lot, a team-building activity, drinks after work, or a five-minute phone conversation about how the week is going, get to know each of them. You need not become best friends, but you should work to build a connection and, through that connection, learn about the work pressures they face.

3. Explain your workplace purpose to them. In particular, use your summary outputs list to talk about your own workplace pressures. Be sure to do this in a nondefensive, matter-of-fact manner. You're not trying to make their demands seem insignificant; rather, your goal is to help them understand the other demands on you, so they have a sense of what their requests look like from your perspective.

Putting your role set "on ICE" helps you establish your trustworthiness with these important people in three ways. First, they learn that you're predictable and come to know what to expect from you when they approach you. Second, they learn that you're reliable and come to believe that you'll follow through when you make a commitment. Third, they learn that you're responsible and come to realize that you keep their agendas in mind even when they don't directly oversee you.[1]

The ICE model is an excellent strategy to employ with your role set no matter what the circumstance. It's especially helpful in the context of crystal building, because it's a way of being overt about your tasks and clear about your relationships. It's your broadcast, and it gives each member of your role set the chance to experience your new cul-

Quick Video: Manage the People Managing You

Visit www.MakeWorkGreat.com for a short video segment about how to use the ICE model (identify, connect, explain) with your role set. This is also an easy bit of information to share if you're trying to describe the contents of this chapter to a trusted friend or colleague.

tural precedents and the associated mutual benefit relationship. This also makes it easy for you to see how receptive each of them is and to note the most receptive ones as natural candidates for enrollment in your new crystal.

One frequent objection to the ICE model is, "So-and-so is in my role set but I don't trust her, so why should I do this?" Notice that there is nothing in the model requiring *you* to trust the other person, only that you become trustworthy *to* her. It is possible to be actually (and visibly) trustworthy to someone you yourself don't trust. Often in the process, mutual trust develops and the relationship improves. If not, you are still the one taking the high road, and you can simply avoid trying to add that person to your crystal for the time being. But to say, "I won't try to be trustworthy to her until she is trustworthy to me" is a bit like standing before a cold fireplace and saying, "I won't give it any wood until it gives me heat."

Broadcast to Your Mentorship Relationships

Do you have a mentor? If not, maybe you should consider finding one.

Are you a mentor to someone else? If not, perhaps you should consider becoming one.

Mentorship relationships take many forms and work on many levels of formality or informality. They can be geared toward the broad-based development of the *mentee* (the person being mentored) or limited to specific skills or information. Not all organizations have formal mentorship programs, yet in almost any group of people with a shared purpose, it's commonplace to find those who have been around longer taking time to share knowledge with the less experienced. This, in fact, is one of the mechanisms by which cultural norms get transferred from person to person in an organization.

Whether the relationship is formal or informal, whether the focus is technical skills or cultural norms, and whether the interaction is short term or long term, all good mentorship relationships have one thing in common: mutual benefit. Not only does the mentee receive an infusion of knowledge from someone who has been there, but the mentor has the chance to share his or her experience in a way that produces specific benefit to someone else and a general benefit to the broader community of which the mentor is a part. Plus, if you've ever tried to teach anyone anything, you know that in the process of doing so you're forced to bring your own expertise to a higher level. In that regard, becoming a mentor builds skills as effectively as having one.

From the perspective of your workplace network, both your mentors and your mentees can make excellent candidates for addition to your crystal. You're already involved in a mutually beneficial relationship, you already have frequent interactions with each other, and you already discuss workplace topics that lend themselves to overtness about task and clarity within relationships. As a practical matter, adding a mentor will be a bit like adding a manager, while adding a mentee will be a bit like adding an employee.

Mutual Benefit: The Ultimate Value Proposition

Did you notice that the notion of mutual benefit comes up consistently in our discussion of potential candidates? Whenever you think about adding someone—an employee, a member of your role set, a mentor, a mentee, or anyone else—to your crystal, it's imperative that you think in terms of mutual benefit.

Why? Certainly, there are valid reasons rooted in ethics and fairness. You can easily imagine the argument that if you're going to be a conscientious creator of culture, you simply must incorporate an element of mutual benefit. To do otherwise—to create a culture of oppression or opportunism—would be irresponsible or "wrong."

Philosophical discussions like this one are worth having. If you're going to change the world around you, it's worth thinking about the kind of world you want to create and live in. These are issues that can be pondered for hours, days, and even lifetimes.

For the moment, consider a simpler and more utilitarian argument for mutual benefit: in attempting to add people to your crystal, you're suggesting that they do things differently. You would like them to interact with you differently and also to role-model overtness and clarity to others. Changes require effort. Think back to our hiring analogy: to successfully hire a new candidate for your company, you must not only convince yourself that he or she is qualified, but also convince the candidate that you're offering a desirable opportunity.

The approach for cultural crystal candidates is the same as the approach for employment candidates. There is an old joke that claims everyone is tuned in to the same radio station—WIIFM, or "What's In It for Me?" There's a bit of cynicism here, but it does work with our broadcast metaphor: the strongest way to suggest that others should make a change is to directly address how the change will help them.

Your new patterns of behavior sell themselves through your actions. As a result of your role-modeling, it becomes obvious to your additions in progress that interacting with you and others in this new way will help them get their own needs met. In asking them through examples and actions to interact with you differently, you're teaching them how to help you to help them even more.

This is why your best candidates come from those closest to you in the workplace network—people like your managers, employees, mentors, mentees, and role set members. You're already in a position to help or support them. In fact, your relationship mandates that you do so. Crystal building must start locally! Imagine how artificial it would be for you to make a contact in another company or industry, attempt to show that person some new patterns of working, and then ask him or her to follow suit. What credibility would you have? What benefit could you offer? How could you say, "Try this, please, and let me know how it goes," or "I think this is the right thing to do"?

Proselytizing in this manner would be uncomfortable for you and detrimental to your new relationship.

By contrast, think of the broadcasting options you have to effect change within the context of relationships in which mutual benefit is already on the table:

- You can explain to an employee that his overtness about resources enables you to support him more effectively: "If you can provide me with a list of the specific help you need, I can work with the management team to get it for you."
- You can seek clarity with your mentor about your need for agreement, which reduces the pressure on her to provide you with the "right" answer: "I value your insight and your opinion. If you would share what you would do in my situation, I'd like to incorporate your experience into my thinking. I realize the final decision of what to do is mine alone, and I'm not asking you to make it for me."
- You can demonstrate the power of overtness about progress by sharing your visibility system with a peer, which increases his confidence in your ability to deliver and seeds the thought of visibility systems for himself: "Just so you know, I use a task tracking system to keep up with my work in progress, including the pieces I owe you. My system keeps me on schedule and ensures that nothing falls through the cracks. If you're interested and it would put your mind at ease, I'd be happy to spend a few minutes showing you my system."

Many other scenarios exist, depending on which part of being overt or seeking clarity you're modeling and your relationship with the other person. Anything you can do to show your candidate that you're making his or her life easier through the application of your new workplace behaviors will go a long way toward enrolling that person in your crystal.

Again, you need not—and should not—envision yourself as a salesperson. We often suspect that salespeople have agendas that run counter to ours, and we tend to approach them with skepticism. But when we discover a useful new product or service on our own, our demeanor is very different. There's no sense of distrust; we're defining our own needs and finding our own solutions. The only feelings are accomplishment and relief.

Your responsibility as a culture builder is not to sell your new cultural patterns, but simply to display and broadcast them. When your additions in progress discover for themselves how useful they are, the change will come willingly and without any selling from you.

Creating Role Models

You may be wondering about the final requirement for members of your cultural crystal. To be considered members, people must not only practice overtness about task and clarity of relationship with you, but role-model them to the rest of their own networks of connections too.

Does this sound like it might be difficult to achieve? At first glance, it goes beyond everything else we have discussed, and you may feel some cynicism about it. Even if you can effect a change in your own relationship with one or more individuals (a tall order in itself), how can you go so far as to change the relationships those individuals have with other people? And all without attempting to "sell" anything? You're not even involved in those relationships!

Prepare yourself. The answer will seem either unbelievable or obvious, depending on how much your crystal has grown when you read this: the change will happen all by itself.

Your new additions will change their interactions with others naturally, because it makes sense to do so. The more effective you are at role-modeling, demonstrating, and implementing overtness and clarity with your additions in progress, the sooner they will realize how practical and helpful those patterns are, and the more quickly they will begin to use them elsewhere in their work lives. When they start to reap the positive benefits of the new patterns with you, they'll naturally look to replicate those same patterns elsewhere to get more of the same.

Your only job is to plant seeds. If a new addition talks about her workplace purpose, you can suggest that she share it with her manager. If you're discussing a different new addition's strongest incentives, you could inquire whether he knows about those of his own employees. Subtly encourage your additions in progress to think in terms of how overtness and clarity could work with the other people in their crystals.

As time goes on, you will find your additions in progress asking questions about how to implement changes with others. This is an indication of growth! Answer those questions and engage in those discussions as fully and positively as you can. Disclose your own successes and mistakes in trying to share your knowledge with others, and complement your new additions about their intentions. If they seem highly receptive, give them copies of this book or share the video lessons it contains. Encourage crystalline growth every chance you get.

Encourage but do *not* force. You won't need to monitor a new addition's relationship with her manager, quiz her about how she talks to her direct reports, or interview her internal or external customers. You needn't ask a recipient of the book whether or not he has read it, and you shouldn't tell him that he'd better get with the program and threaten to withhold your support if he doesn't. Focus only on the relationships between you and your new additions. Let conversations about how they manage their other relationships come up in due course and at their pace, not yours. Impatience may tempt you to push forward more quickly, but rest assured, this is contrary to your goals.

Remember, crystalline growth is an organic process, like the growth of a plant. To get flowers, you plant seeds, provide sunlight and water, and leave the rest to Mother Nature. To grow a cultural crystal, you become a seed crystal of positive workplace behaviors, encourage others to connect with you, and leave the rest to human nature. You don't serve your desire for roses by digging up the earth each week to see what the seeds are doing, and you don't serve your desire for cultural change by nosily involving yourself in other people's relationships. If you have picked the right person and done a good job role-modeling and encouraging, then growth will occur in its own time.

Organic Growth

How do I know this will happen? Consider the simple elegance at work here. Your additions in progress are people you selected as being both capable and receptive. Having learned something about overtness and clarity from you, they will eventually notice a single instance elsewhere in their work lives where one of these different patterns might be useful. Perhaps one will realize that clarifying the need for agreement will help with a difficult customer. Perhaps another will decide that overtness about capability will be useful in sharing information with a new manager. Sooner or later, such realizations will come.

When they do, it's almost certain that your new additions won't think of themselves as "attempting cultural change." Rather, they will be trying to create a positive outcome for themselves. As a result, they will automatically select a situation with a high likelihood for success. Remember, you selected them because they are highly capable. And because they learned the new patterns through your role-modeled examples, they will be even more flexible and targeted in their application of them than you are. (This is to your credit: you had to learn the patterns at least in part from a book; they had the benefit of seeing you demonstrate them in real life.)

This means they are likely to use their new patterns successfully and receive positive encouragement in the form of the results they wanted. This reinforces two notions: the idea that the new pattern should be used again, and the idea that their relationship with you is a source of positive, useful information. Both of these lessons will accelerate their next attempt to try another new pattern. Organic growth takes care of itself.

What if their first attempts fail? Perhaps, to stay with our examples, a difficult customer gets more difficult or a new manager is unreceptive. If fledgling attempts don't work out as intended, does it mean the loss of any hope that your additions in progress might continue to learn and practice the new cultural patterns?

Probably not. Remember, you're not putting yourself in a position of telling these people what to do with respect to overtness and clarity. Rather, you're role-modeling your patterns and allowing them to learn by example. The difference here is substantial: if you told an addition in progress to do something, and it didn't work, then you were wrong and they will think twice before listening to you and your crazy ideas again. But if your additions in progress discover the importance of overtness and clarity through observation, determine on their own that they might help, and develop their own strategies for implementation, then they have no reason to doubt your credibility! If anything, they may come back to you to share their stories if things go wrong, giving both of you the opportunity to learn from their experiences. Since you're role-modeling many patterns and providing lots of content to help your additions in progress develop their own strategies, you retain your advisory function.

No strategy is perfect, but organic systems are self-correcting. Remember what happens when a branch of a rosebush bumps into a wall. The plant doesn't die, it simply adjusts. Organic growth takes care of itself.

Selective Versus Exclusive

As we close this chapter, one other aspect of the organic growth process is worthy of attention: the difference between selectivity and exclusivity.

Let's return once again to the metaphor of ice formation on a pond. Consider for a moment the type of "screening" that goes on from the perspective of the growing ice crystal. As the new crystal takes form, it sits there silently encouraging neighboring particles to attach. You might imagine particles of the emerging crystal saying, "Look at this. I'm doing this, and you can be a part of it." The broadcast is a positive invitation to change, not an attempt to force or sell. Any neighboring particle that is able to do so can quickly attach.

In the moment, some particles attach and others don't because some are ready and others are not. Particles that are receptive to the change—adjacent surface molecules at the freezing temperature—join quickly. Unreceptive particles—those underwater and at slightly higher temperatures—are left unchanged. That's all. They're not blacklisted, rejected, thrown out, excluded, or ostracized. They're simply left unchanged.

Ice formation is selective but not exclusive. Our anthropomorphized ice crystal would not be heard saying, "Well, I'm not so sure about you. You meet the criteria, but I really don't want you around." Nor would we hear, "Nope. I invited you an hour ago, and you said you weren't ready, so you missed your chance." Only those particles able to make the change are allowed to do so, but all of them are allowed to do so. Whenever an adjacent particle is "ready," it's admitted.

This is an important lesson in growing a cultural crystal. So far, this book has suggested that you be selective about whom you consider for inclusion. You must choose people you judge to be capable, ethical, and receptive; people with whom you are already connected; people with whom you have a high potential for mutually beneficial relationships. This selectivity is important, as you assess who is prepared to enroll.

On the other hand, you must take care not to let selectivity turn into exclusivity. You're building a culture, not a clique or a cult; this is "Make Work Great," not "Make Work Homogeneous"! If you begin to include additional, more personal criteria in your selection process, it will change the nature of what you're doing. Attempts to create an "inner circle" of those who dress, act, or think alike may provide the opportunity to assuage your insecurities or correct the social injustices of your youth, but they don't produce beneficial changes in the broader culture around you. If anything, they encourage a division between those who are "in" and those who are "out." This creates a dysfunctional social dynamic, as people must then make decisions relative to that division: "Do I try to get in?" "Am I proudly out?" and so forth. Engaging people in this way improves neither output nor enjoyment; instead, it fills the workplace with pubescent antics and personal dramas.

As you begin to build your funnel model (see Figure 5.3), beware of the difference between selectivity and exclusivity. Be ruthlessly selective in spending your time and energy on those who will be interested in your new patterns and able to notice your example and make use of it. At the same time, be widely inclusive in who you consider. Don't go looking for yes-men, social climbers, or those who calm your doubts through their words or actions. Instead, seek anyone who is capable, competent, and ready to learn. In doing so, you'll be building a crystal that is stable, diverse, and sustainable over the long term.

EXERCISES

1. In your role-modeling so far, who around you has been particularly receptive to your new patterns of behavior at work? Are any of these people candidates for addition to your cultural crystal? How many candidates do you have at this point?

2. Consider the funnel model in Figure 5.3. Are you ready to work a bit harder with one or two more individuals as additions in progress? Think carefully about how many you can handle at one time and remember your limit. Be careful not to overload yourself: it's far better to succeed on a small scale than to flounder on a grand one.

3. If you have identified a second person as a potential addition in progress, review the guidelines in Chapter 4 that correspond to your relationship with that person (employee, manager, or peer). Make a plan for the first thing you'll do to engage with your second addition in progress.

6 When Growth Is Difficult

This all sounds ideal, doesn't it? You're going to allow people to add themselves to your cultural crystal, a few at a time, by role-modeling new cultural patterns to those who are most receptive to them. Don't worry about the difficult people, and don't worry about making mistakes. Just do it, and keep doing it. Will the rest really take care of itself?

Actually, to a large extent, it will. The more frequently and consistently you demonstrate the new patterns to the people around you, the more you encourage your additions in progress to become culture demonstrators themselves, and the more diligently you hold yourself to your new, higher standards of behavior, the more results you'll see. This is an organic process, like ice formation or plant growth. If the conditions are correct, success is the natural outcome.

It sounds very promising. Yet if you've worked with other human beings, you know how problematic interactions can be, and you know that the best intentions and plans can quickly go terribly wrong. So you may find yourself hopeful but feeling you'd be a little more comfortable if you had some answers to your questions. These questions probably begin with the phrase "What do I do if . . ." and end with statements of calamity such as "my boss won't listen," "my peer gets angry," or "my direct report calls me an obscene name." If you're feeling this sort of cautious optimism, you're ready for this chapter, the last in our section about growing your cultural crystal. Here, you'll find tools to help with the difficulties you'll face as your crystal develops.

Making It a Habit

Let's start where we always start—with you. The biggest challenge you face in creating and growing your cultural crystal will most likely not come from difficult coworkers, impossibly inflexible management, or a disengaged and disinterested employee base. It will far more likely come from you.

This stems from the nature of our approach. This is not a one-time, high-impact, visible change that you implement, deploy, or inflict on your organization. Rather, it is a set of subtle, incremental changes in your own work that together launch the organic process of improvement in your environment. It is not the construction of a shade structure, but the planting of an oak seed. It is not liposuction, but a small change in eating and exercise patterns. (There is no judgment intended regarding the appropriateness of shade structures, liposuction, or any other human-made process—just a reminder that these are not the patterns we are attempting to follow.)

The good news—in the sense of what you have to do today, tomorrow, and next week—is that this is a much easier way to influence the culture around you. There's no constituent support, deployment plan, or executive buy-in needed; no formal launch to plan. You can simply start, as soon as this minute and as small as you like. The other side of the coin, however, is that for the organic process to take hold, you have to be consistent and make the change in a permanent way. You have to demonstrate your new behaviors today, tomorrow, next week, next month, next quarter, and next year.

In other words, your practice of overtness about task and clarity within relationship must become habitual. To do what this book suggests, you must develop some new habits. If you're having problems implementing your new cultural patterns, start by considering the strength of those habits.

How can you most easily create or strengthen a habit? Much has been written about this topic, and current researchers don't agree on the mechanics of habit formation.[1] However, academics and popular psychologists alike seem to agree that some basic ingredients are required to form a new habit.[2–4]

First, some connection between the intended action and a desirable goal is necessary. In this case, you need to believe that the practices of overtness and clarity will lead to positive outcomes at work. Reading this book is a start, and experimenting with your own new patterns of behavior is the next step. As you begin to experience positive outcomes, pay special attention to even your smallest successes; perhaps reserve some pages in your notebook to chronicle the positive results you see. In doing so, the connection between action and goal will become stronger in your own mind.

Second, some type of cuing or reminder system is helpful at the beginning. You might write a note in your calendar to begin each meeting with your manager by reciting your summary outputs list, or you can ask a close friend to remind you to do so as you enter the meeting. The reminder may be useful for your next 5, 10, or 20 meetings. Sooner or later, the behavior will become habitual and the reminder unnecessary.

Third, a time frame for intentionally repeating manageable changes is useful. Some physical trainers advise new clients to exercise a little every single day for their first 30 to 45 days, because this approach is far more likely to create a new habit than a few arduous workouts per week. In the context of crystal building, the idea of such repetition suggests that it's not to your advantage to try to do everything differently tomorrow. Rather, it's better to make only a small change—perhaps picking one form of overtness or clarity—and stick with it every single day for at least a month.

The combination of these three fundamentals of habit is powerful. For instance, you may decide that you'd like to improve your clarity of approach by spending a little more time preparing for potentially difficult interactions in advance. To do so, you might place a note on your dashboard that says, "Consider your approach." Then you might spend

Creating or Strengthening a Habit

- Form and strengthen the connection between the desired action and the positive result it will generate by taking specific note of your expected and actual successes.
- Develop a cuing system to remind you to repeat your new behavior at regular intervals. Try to find a cue that will become a natural stimulus in the future, one that's connected with the desired outcome.
- Set a time frame for repetition (such as daily for four to six weeks), and make a conscious effort to follow it.

the first five minutes of your daily commute pondering and defining your approach to a specific individual with whom you're planning to converse that day. After 30 days, you'll likely find yourself being cued at the start of your commute to think more consciously about the approaches you'll employ for your most important interactions that day.

Of course, this is just one example, and you must choose what will work for you. The key is to understand that you'll begin with an *action-outcome pattern* in which you take specific action because you're motivated by the outcome you'll achieve. This requires conscious effort. Through repetition and using the elements mentioned here, you will eventually move to a *stimulus-response pattern.* In this pattern, a given stimulus (such as lack of overtness about the purpose of a meeting) will lead to an appropriate habitual response on your part (such as asking about the need for agreement). This is when your new habit will be cemented, so that in the future it will require a lot less conscious attention.[5] This also might be the best time to choose another new form of task overtness or relationship clarity, and begin the habit-building process again.

As you form your new habits, resist the temptation to come up with a deadline by which you expect to see certain results. No clairvoyant formula exists to tell you how many days, weeks, months, or quarters it will take for your new behaviors to become precedents in the crystal around you. Indeed, you would be wise to be suspicious of such a formula if it were presented. So many variables are at play—what you do, how consistently you do it, how receptive your coworkers are, what other changes are happening around you, what it would take for you to perceive a change, and so on—that there can be no single meaningful answer to how long it will take, other than "It depends."

Besides, while the question of the time involved is tempting to ask, you must admit that it's a lot like asking, "How much exercise must I do before I'm fit and I can stop?" Emma (my supervisor from Chapter 1) did not set out early in her career to create an environment that would allow one of her employees to solve a specific problem years later and then stop after it happened! She consistently practiced the disciplines of overtness and clarity, so that she and her team were well positioned for challenges as they arose.

Building a cultural crystal is not a project with an end date but a process you keep practicing for your own good as much as for the good of your environment.

Troubleshooting Interactions

"That's fine," you may be saying. "I can work on my own habits all day long, but *my* biggest problem isn't going to be me. *My* biggest problem is someone else!" At this point, you utter the name of the most problematic, thorny, difficult person in your workplace, and you say it with the biggest scowl and most negative intonation you can muster. So-and-so is a thorn in your side, and he or she will be a problem.

Because much of the training in my consulting practice focuses on optimizing information transfer, I often ask session participants to discuss in general terms someone who is driving them crazy at work. Poor communication equals poor information transfer, and these troublesome people are our real-life case studies. It's a great topic to bring up when a group's energy is low; I have never found a question that leads to livelier conversation. Everyone seems to have at least one difficult person at work and to be able to recount the pain associated with that person quickly and emotionally. Some of these interpersonal issues are beyond any hope of improvement, but many others can be salvaged through the conscious action of one of the parties involved.

In this chapter, we'll address both cases—the person with whom some progress is possible and the one with whom all hope is lost. But be warned, everything to follow is really just a rephrasing of the message you've already read. If you create good habits of overtness and clarity and use them consistently, much of the rest will take care of itself. The practice of your good habits is the first—and most important—tactic you can use when dealing with any difficult situation.

The Most Difficult Person

Let's start with the worst-case scenario. There are a few people in your work life who are hopeless. You know it. They're not going to be receptive to any changes you make; they're certainly not interested in making the workplace better; and just maybe, they're out to get you a little. What do you do when there's no getting through, no improving, and no hope? How can you effect a cultural change when some of the people around you simply won't move?

The answer is deceptively simple, and we have already discussed it: ignore them.

Let's qualify that a little. Obviously, since you work with these people, you must interact with them. Although it may sound tempting, ignoring them doesn't mean giving them the silent treatment or the cold shoulder, or refusing to take their calls or answer their e-mails. Remember, nothing in this book is suggesting that you stop doing what your job requires. Stay successful, engaged, and ethical.

Yet purely from the perspective of effecting cultural change, you can (and should) completely ignore them. Waste no time in attempting to explain what you're doing or to convince them of anything. Leave them in the "everyone around me" section of your funnel model. They may or may not notice that you're practicing some new patterns of overtness and clarity. Remember the distinction between being selective and being exclusive. Don't become judgmental, don't treat them badly, and don't become cliquish in your handling of them. Don't exclude them, but don't select them either. Do what you do, and let them do what they do. Conduct business as you must, but don't waste any culture-changing energy that could be better spent elsewhere in your crystal.

What if this difficult person is your boss, your employee, or your customer? How can you possibly hope to change the culture around you if you can't even change that one person? The answer is time. Consider the scenario represented in Figure 6.1. You have made no changes with your "impossible" person, but you have managed over time to successfully add three other members to your cultural crystal. One of those members has even successfully added a single member of his or her own.

Notice what has happened. Although you haven't improved your interaction with the impossible person, he or she is now receiving role-modeled examples of your new cultural patterns from four different individuals. By focusing your attention elsewhere, you've begun to successfully "wrap" your new culture around that one difficult person.

Imagine a chunk of granite protruding from the surface of a lake that's in the process of freezing over. Granite is a different structure,

Effective Behavioral Change

One particularly effective approach to promoting behavioral change in both animals and humans is the act of ignoring undesired behaviors while consistently rewarding desired ones.[6] The crystal-wrapping approach presented here amounts to a system-level implementation of that same strategy: you are providing positive reinforcement in the form of enhanced mutual benefit to those people who are able to attach to your crystal and not wasting any energy trying to penalize or change those who are unable to do so.

FIGURE 6.1 Wrapping an impossible person

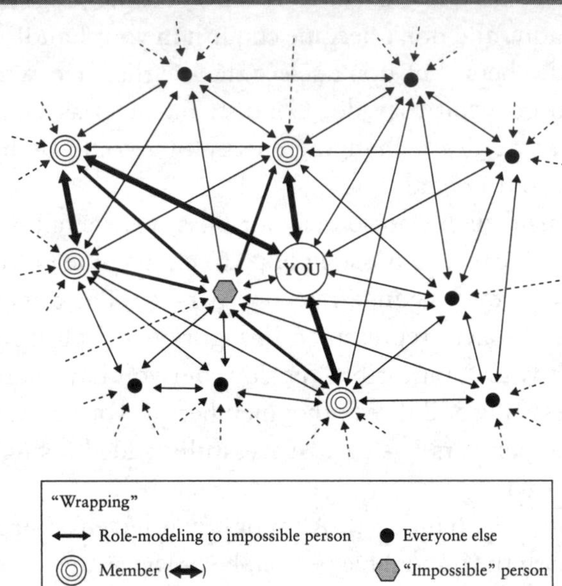

and it will simply not convert into frozen water. As nearby particles of water attach to the ice crystal and change their form, they spend no energy trying to encourage the granite to do so. The new crystal simply wraps around the granite, leaving it to exist as it sees fit in the newly changed environment.

Notice the wrapping effect at work in Figure 6.1. One of the individuals who is role-modeling to your impossible person is someone with whom you don't have a direct link. As your crystal members add their own new members, the most resistant people begin to experience more and more role-modeled examples of the new cultural patterns from people who don't even interact with you on any regular basis.

This is why it works to ignore the difficult people around you and focus on the more pleasant ones. In enrolling new members where you can, you ultimately end up influencing your most difficult coworkers without ever dealing with them directly. All it takes is the consistent practice of your good habits.

The Somewhat Difficult Person

What about people who, on your desirable-to-difficult scale, fall somewhere in the middle? They may not be your favorite people in the world, but you do have some positive interactions with them. You also think you could begin to role-model at least certain types of overtness and clarity to them and perhaps someday be able to include them in your crystal. On one hand, they might make (somewhat tenuous) additions in progress; on the other hand, you have had your share of difficulty with them. Should you proceed?

To answer that question, you need to be painfully honest with yourself about your intent. Why do you want to add one of these people to your crystal? Ask yourself directly and reflect on the answer. You may find you want to "bring that person around," teach that person something that will "do him or her good," or something similar. If you're trying to change the other person this way, even if you have the best possible broader goals, you should abandon your quest. Refocus your attention on the creation and maintenance of other members of your crystal where success is more likely.

Why? Recall the mechanics of the organic process you're employing. The whole system depends on other people discovering, in their own time, that by interacting with you according to the new patterns you're demonstrating, they realize a greater benefit. If you go into the situation trying to change a person, you'll be much more likely to try to direct him or her, obviously or covertly, to act the way you want. The person is no longer faced with the question "What's in it for me?" but with the question "Should I do what I'm being told?" You may or may not be successful in getting compliance, but you're unlikely to inspire organic crystalline growth.*

---

*Of course there is nothing inherently wrong with attempting to change someone's behavior appropriately. If you are in a managerial role, for example, it is your responsibility to set performance expectations for your employees and to hold them accountable to those expectations. Taking this a step further, you could set expectations with your staff regarding overtness of task and clarity of relationships. Just remember that until your employees are able to perceive benefit to themselves from what they are doing, there will be no further organic growth beyond compliance with your directives.

What if your intentions are pure? Perhaps you don't want to change the occasionally difficult person, but you believe you can successfully create mutual benefit by role-modeling your new cultural patterns. You're a little hesitant to try because of some past communication difficulties between you. Perhaps you also sense that both of you had a role in those difficulties, and you wonder what improvements you could make that would help. In that case, you might benefit from the following model for troubleshooting the inevitable difficult patches in your communication.

Five Building Blocks of Reality

"Why am I having such a hard time communicating with this person?" Most of us ask that question in silent (or not-so-silent) frustration, as we struggle through a conflict over what we think should be a simple issue. Phrases like "How can you not see it this way?" and "You don't seem to understand," have their roots in honest confusion about the source of disagreement but quickly become points of argument all their own. Conflict builds on conflict until the original

Conflict in the Crystalline Network

Conflict is another interpersonal field about which much has been written. Daniel Katz long ago suggested three sources of conflict: conflict over scarce resources, conflict over incompatible ideology, and conflict over competing desire for power or influence.[7] Ron Fisher adds the possibility of conflict driven by miscommunication.[8] Analysis of issues related to the importance of an individual's role set led Katz and Robert Kahn to consider causes of conflict such as role conflict, role overload, and issues of perception between the senders and receivers of expectations.[9] Roger Fisher and William Ury promote the need to separate the people, positions, and interests and deal with them separately.[10] My five building blocks of reality are based on the commonalities among these and other related sources.

point of discussion is lost among secondary bones of contention. It's a place we've all been and a hard one from which to return, especially when the pressure to come to an agreement is strong.

What causes these disagreements? Why do some people have to struggle so hard to see our version of reality and vice versa? In part, it's because our definition of reality often includes more components than we realize.

Let's take a simple example. Imagine yourself attending a presentation about company revenue. You see it, think about it, and decide what it means. This seems simple, but as Figure 6.2 indicates, five building blocks actually make up your reality; in other words, five components of your experience get you from the information "out there" to the reality you experience as your own.

Start on the left with the most objective of the five building blocks: information. Notice that the figure includes both the factual content and the person presenting it. The factual information, the way it's displayed, how well it's explained, and the presenter's nonverbal communication cues are all part of this component. This information is the initial stimulus you receive that leads you to your version of "reality." It's your starting point, but not your whole journey.

FIGURE 6.2 The five building blocks of reality

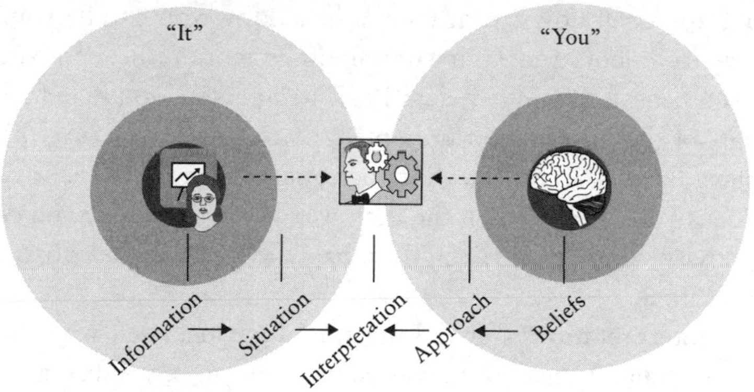

Connected to the information is the situation, which is the surrounding context. Is the information being presented by a neutral third party or by someone who has a personal interest in your reaching a certain conclusion? Is there a historical context? Are there any other surrounding facts? The social context—who is in the room at the time, your role, and the roles of the others—is also important. Who is there, and how much interest do they have in soliciting specific responses from others who are present? Revenue summaries made publicly to shareholders by CEOs contain the same facts and figures as those made privately to CEOs by CFOs. They do not necessarily impart the same message.

Now look at the right end of the model and consider your deepest beliefs. In the figure, they are represented by your brain, though if it were possible to produce a drawing of your hidden thoughts and values, that would be more appropriate. Your beliefs are the most difficult component for anyone, yourself included, to perceive. They include assumptions about things like survival, community, and what you see as important. Often they are unexplored and unquestioned. A strong unspoken belief in the longevity of your company, for example, will mitigate your perception of the seriousness of a slow economic year, while a deep-seated concern about the company's direction will have the opposite effect. Questions of philosophy also come into play here. Do you consider your company's primary role to be the production of products or shareholder value?

Your approach flows from your beliefs. How you handle your job, your environment, and your surroundings is more observable than what you believe. If you're a detail-oriented person, you may focus on one part of the information presented; if you're a big-picture thinker, you may take it as an overview. If you equate money with security, you may focus your attention on the net revenue or reserves; if you equate productivity with security, you'll probably focus more heavily on output indicators.

Your interpretation is at the meeting point between what is "out there" and what is inside you. It is yours alone; in it, you bring to bear all of your experiences, knowledge, and ways of thinking about the world, and you internalize your ideas about what you perceive. When considering the revenue report, you may be optimistic or pessimistic. You may decide the information is valid or suspect. You may take it at face value or wish to apply statistical analysis to the data. All of these are decisions of interpretation, as you answer the question "What does this mean to me?"

As you can see from this simple example, the five building blocks of reality are as interconnected as they are separate. The information stands alone, yet it is part of the situation; your approach and the pressures you face exist in advance, yet they're influenced by both your beliefs and your interpretation. Each of the building blocks of your reality is influenced by the others, especially those closest to it.

Discuss What You're Discussing

Figure 6.3 shows an enlargement of an interaction between two people, complete with the building blocks for each. When we add another person who is reviewing the same company revenue presentation you

FIGURE 6.3 Sample interaction in terms of the five building blocks of reality

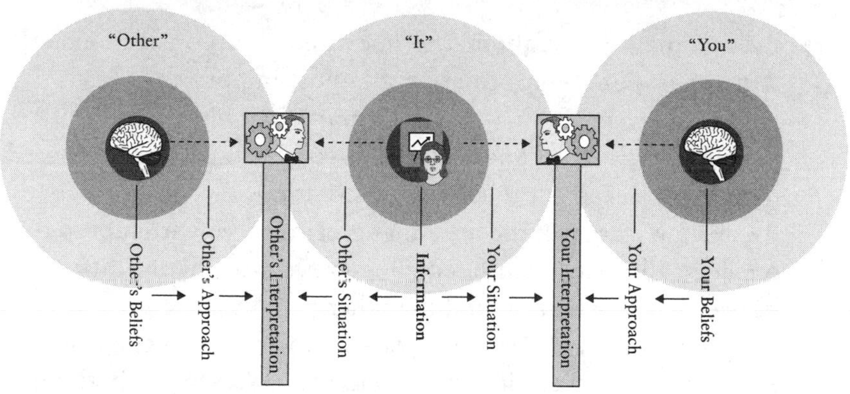

are, it becomes obvious that each of the five building blocks is a possible area of contention. You may be looking at the same information, but each of you has your own situation, interpretation, approach, and beliefs about it.

This often leads to disagreement and conflict, because the topic of your discussion rarely reflects the actual area of divergence. You and the other person might have a disagreement about the correct conclusions to be drawn from the revenue presentation. The real root of your disagreement may be situation, interpretation, approach, or belief, but if your conversation keeps revolving around the information or topic—in this case, company revenue—frustration will build and the exchange of actual information will deteriorate. After all, you can't solve a dispute between interpretations or beliefs by arguing over information. "It obviously means this," and "No, it doesn't!" is about as far as you'll get.

The solution is as difficult as it is obvious: when disagreement arises, discuss the real reason for the conflict! That is, use the five building blocks of reality to keep the topic of your conversation aligned with the source of your conflict. If the disagreement is over interpretation, discuss interpretation. If the disagreement is over belief, discuss belief. And so on.

Of course, it is your own habitual practice of overtness and clarity that prepares you to do this:

- By seeking clarity about the question, you consider exactly which parts of the information are most important to you.
- By being overt about your own purpose, impact, incentive, progress, resources, and capability, you become fully prepared to explain the constraints of your situation.
- By seeking clarity of the need for agreement, you attempt to reconcile in advance the different pressures caused by the difference between your situation and the other person's.
- By seeking clarity of approach, you seek to avoid unspoken, unnecessary conflicts over differences in the approaches you both take.

In much the same way you wrap your cultural crystal around a difficult person, you are "wrapping" your preparation around the question of interpretation. You can't predict someone else's interpretation, but you can prepare for what it might be.

Of course, difficult situations require flexibility. If you find yourself lost in conflict, one easy tactic may help you recover: just step through each building block, one by one, starting with information.

Begin with *information* because it is the most objective place to start. Open a new conversation by discussing what you need to discuss. This will include your preparation regarding clarity of the question. By opening with the goal of the interaction and the information required, you first address the question of whether you're talking about the right things, so that it doesn't muddle the discussion that follows. A well-defined question at this step can save a lot of effort later in the exchange.

Now move to *situation*. Here, agreement is more likely if you share what you perceive and encourage the other person to do the same: "Let's take a moment to discuss the situational considerations. Here are the contextual factors from my point of view. What are yours?" By taking an inquisitive, nonjudgmental stance toward the other person's perceptions, you can build a shared context for understanding the information itself. This is where clarity of the need for agreement enters and where both of you increase your understanding of the other's role pressures.

As you move into *interpretation*, you enter a more private, more subjective space. As you do, remember that "Here's my interpretation. What do you think?" is a much more useful approach than "Here's my interpretation and why it's right." Seek to understand and be understood, rather than to convince. If you're lucky, this will be as far as you need to go. At this point, you'll be able to return to your well-defined question and find an answer to it by considering the commonalities between multiple interpretations.

If disagreement persists, move next to questions of *approach*. Again, these conversations are best framed in exploratory terms rather than dictatorial ones. Start with a tentative explanation of your own approach and then respectfully request the other person's response: "I've been called a detail person. Do you see this as a situation where more detailed analysis is needed?" Remember that the two of you can agree to disagree regarding your preferred approach and yet still come to a conclusion on your well-defined question.

The final building block, *belief*, is the most difficult to address. If discussion of the first four blocks leads to conclusion, be happy that you can avoid this level. We're not always fully aware of the beliefs that drive our own actions, much less those that underlie someone else's. Still, if you're pestered by a consistent disagreement beneath the surface of your conversation, beliefs may be worth exploring. Again, one way is to role-model your own disclosure. "I always tend to silently assume something," you might say. "I'm thinking that belief may be at play here, so let me share it with you and see what you think." By demonstrating your own openness, you may encourage the other person to return the favor.

This Is Hard!

Obviously, no magic strategy can guarantee successful interactions. Nothing in what we have discussed precludes the other person from being difficult—our troubleshooting model specifies only what you can do. Discussing what you're discussing won't work every time, but generally it improves the quality and quantity of information flowing in both directions and prevents certain unimportant differences from becoming sticking points. It takes extra time and effort, but it does become easier with practice. Whether you get the skill from a book, a mentor, or a coach, you will undoubtedly find value in the ability to consciously isolate the various components of what was previously a knee-jerk response and then address them appropriately.

On the other hand, while the application of this model to any troublesome interaction might produce some good results, don't lose sight of your primary goal. From a culture-change perspective, this isn't

Quick Video: Disagree, Don't Argue

Visit www.MakeWorkGreat.com for a short video segment about how to use the five building blocks of reality to improve your communications. This is also an easy bit of information to share if you're trying to describe the contents of this chapter to a trusted friend or colleague.

your only option. You can also choose to wrap your crystal around the other person. If you're already practicing good habits regarding overtness and clarity, yet you still find yourself in frequent, painful, and/or unrecoverable disagreements with someone, then that person is probably not a great candidate for addition to your crystal at the moment.

In that case, look back at Figure 6.1, reassure yourself that you can influence this person more effectively by focusing your attention on someone else, and move on in your culture-changing efforts. Use the troubleshooting model for situations in which it helps, but don't waste energy trying to convert someone who simply isn't interested. Keep practicing your good habits, and turn your attention elsewhere when you can.

Life on the Boundary

By now, you should have realized that for the foreseeable future you're going to be interacting with two kinds of people—those who reciprocate your new patterns of interaction and those who don't. The idealized distant future may contain a reality in which every person around you is a member of your cultural crystal, but the immediate outlook is probably not so ideal.

That's okay! We've discussed in detail how to handle the different categories of people—members, additions in progress, candidates for addition, and everyone else. We've reviewed a troubleshooting

Culture Building with Difficult People

- For the most difficult, focus elsewhere and allow your cultural crystal to wrap around them slowly.
- For the moderately difficult, prepare yourself first, using overtness about task and clarity about relationship.
- During the discussion, separate the five building blocks of reality (information, situation, interpretation, approach, and beliefs) and address each separately.

model for handling difficult interactions. We've also discussed wrapping your crystal around the most problematic individuals. Only one topic remains as we conclude the section on growing your crystal: preparing yourself for life on the boundary.

At the beginning, you saw a better way to work before anyone else did. You had to encourage yourself to "choose to choose" in the face of so much contrary role-modeling. That was difficult enough. But now you're in an even more complex situation. You're practicing better patterns of working with some of your coworkers, while others are unwilling to go there with you.

That is life on the boundary, and it's your new normal. As a culture builder, you will spend your work life connected with some people according to your new patterns of overtness and clarity, and with others according to the old patterns that existed before (perhaps feeling as though you're role-modeling to a brick wall). You will be the one who most strongly feels the pull between the two ways of working. The dichotomy will exist in your work life every day and every hour. If you don't see this as a natural part of your role, it can be quite stressful.

Make no mistake: the dichotomy *is* a natural part of your role. As the culture builder, you will always be pulled forward toward the change you're trying to make and backward toward the way things have always been. Which of the two influences feels stronger will depend on the day, who is in the room with you, and your own state of mind. The reason this book began with the mandate to choose to choose, the reason it advocates small changes in specific patterns of your behavior, and the reason it focuses on your formation of strong habits is because those are the tools that keep you on track, even when the pressure to fall backward gets strong.

At times, that pressure will likely get intense. The people who follow your lead, especially early on, will be in the minority, while those who don't wish to change can be quite obvious about it. And those who are change-averse speak and act with all the alleged authority of the organization's shared memory: "It doesn't matter that this could be more productive, easier, or more pleasant. It's not how we do things around here!" They are all influenced by the members of their own role sets, more people encouraging them not to change. Remind yourself in these situations that the alleged authority is based on nothing more than what someone else did accidentally in the past.

As you progress, you will feel the ebb and flow of this reverse pull. In addition to your well-formed, consistent habits of practicing overtness and clarity, four other strategies may help you keep moving forward when your life on the boundary becomes challenging.

First, don't expect too much. If you expect your whole environment to embrace your new ideas with open arms, you're setting yourself up for disappointment. One excellent reason to try for small victories first is so that you can build up your confidence in your new patterns of behavior. Your habits—your "inner game"—matter most. Don't rely on external reinforcement to believe that you're making intelligent changes. Instead, rely on your habit structures: action-outcome and stimulus-response.

Second, keep track. Using your notebook to maintain a list of members, additions in progress, and candidates is a great idea. You can use the worksheet at the end of this chapter for that purpose. Just be sure to keep your lists private and be diligent in your intention to stay selective but not exclusive.

Third, avoid preaching. You may be tempted to extol the virtues of your new behaviors to a broad audience. Avoid this inclination! Dogmatism doesn't promote organic growth; in fact, it is counter to it. At best, if you're a powerful figure, it produces blind conformity. At worst, it produces nothing but conflict and turns its most vocal proponents into targets.

Finally, accept nonlinear progress. If you expect that today you'll see a teeny change, a slightly larger one tomorrow, a still-larger change the next day, and so forth, you'll be disappointed. Organic processes develop in fits and starts. Visible plant growth is nonlinear, and lakes don't freeze from left to right in 10 percent increments. What you're more likely to see is prolonged periods of little visible change followed by bursts of improvement.

It is no accident that these four strategies would work equally well under the heading of "practicing good habits." As we close this section about growing your crystal, take a moment to notice once again that your practice of good cultural habits is the key to your success at creating growth and making work great. Whether you are collaborating with receptive individuals, handling difficult people, or dealing with the pressures of your life on the cultural boundary, the consistent and effective application of overtness about task and clarity within relationship is the key to your success.

Add to that a little patience, and the rest will follow naturally.

Existing on the Boundary Between Cultures

- Don't expect too much too soon.
- Keep track of your growing crystal.
- Avoid preaching or dogmatism.
- Accept nonlinear progress.

EXERCISES

1. Choose one form of overtness or clarity that you would like to make into a habit. Then consider how you can apply each of the three key elements of a habit:

   a. Write a short description of why practicing this specific behavior will be beneficial. What will be the positive outcome for you?
   b. Select a specific cue that will remind you to practice that behavior—perhaps a note in your calendar, an alarm, or some other physical reminder.
   c. Set a time horizon of four to six weeks during which you commit to practicing the new behavior every day. Your goal is to move from an action-outcome habit to a stimulus-response habit.

---

2. Consider a potentially difficult interaction you face over the next several days, perhaps involving someone with whom you have had conflicts in the past. Using Figure 6.2 as a guide, try to identify your five building blocks of reality and how each of yours differs from the other person's. Can you predict the most likely area of conflict?

---

3. When you have the difficult interaction, keep a watchful eye on not only the content of your discussion, but also on the building block that matters. Try to make sure that the actual discussion is aligned with the covert source of conflict at all times. Note: If you have a trusting relationship with the other person, you may even consider sharing Figure 6.2, explaining what you're trying to do, and seeking his or her help.

---

4. Create a duplicate of the worksheet in Figure 6.4 for use in your notebook. Begin tracking the individual members of your crystal, the additions in progress, and the candidates and non-candidates in your environment. Take care to keep your notes private.

FIGURE 6.4 Worksheet for tracking your crystal-building plans and progress

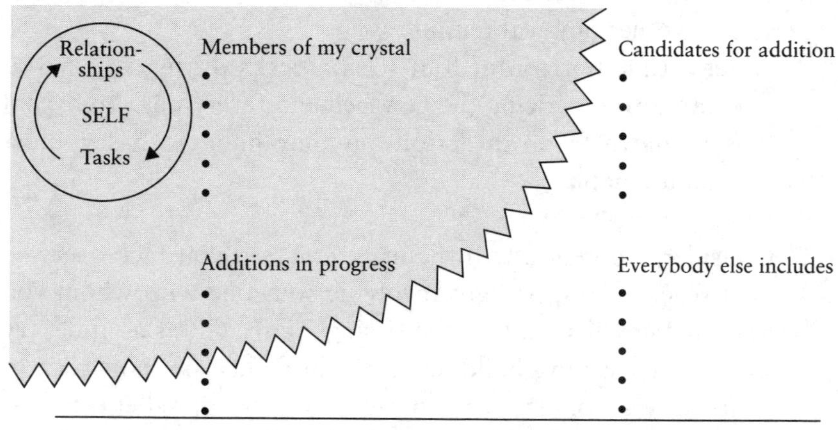

Practicing Overtness and Clarity

Overtness About Task
- Workplace purpose
- Impact of my work
- My incentives
- My progress (visibility systems)
- Resources needed
- Capability I need

Clarity About Relationship
- Define the question
- Define the approach
- Define the need for agreement

Remember

- Be selective, not exclusive
- Focus on the easy additions
- Make my members as successful as possible

PART 3

LEADING YOUR CRYSTAL

One of the hardest tasks of leadership is understanding that you are not what you are, but what you're perceived to be by others.

—EDWARD L. FLOM

7 From Contributor to Advisor

Imagine a large cage housing five monkeys. A ladder in the center leads up to a tasty bunch of bananas. But each time a monkey attempts to climb the ladder, an experimenter stops it with a spray of ice-cold water at high pressure. In the process, the primates that aren't climbing the ladder also feel the punishing effect of the icy spray. Soon, the five monkeys learn to steer clear of the ladder, ignore the bananas, and go about their lives in the rest of the cage.

Now imagine removing one of the monkeys and replacing it with a new one. Naturally, the newcomer gravitates toward the ladder and its tasty prize. But the other four know better. To protect themselves from the harsh spray, they take action to prevent the newcomer's ascent. Their actions are hostile and physical—monkeys don't have meetings, after all—and successful. After a few thwarted attempts and a few new bruises, the recent initiate learns to live like the others, all but ignoring the ladder and its prize.

This metaphor is often employed to explain the irrational pull of policy and precedent in organizations. The animals can be replaced slowly, one at a time, until the cage houses five monkeys who have never felt the spray of icy water, yet they will not allow each other to climb to the bananas even if the experimenter departs and the threat is removed. Most often, this story is presented as an experimental result, although it may well be an urban myth.

Either way, the punch line is compelling: "That's just how we do things around here." Many of us can relate to this workplace experience—trying to do something so obviously sensible and in return being beaten up by those around us for no rational reason beyond a vague reference to policy.

For our purposes, let's treat our monkey story as a fable and take it a little further. Imagine now that one of the five newcomers takes a different approach. Rather than making a beeline for the bananas and suffering the wrath of the others, our chosen one wanders over to the ladder one day and stands nearby—just stands there—for a moment, before moving on. Then she repeats this behavior over time, progressively spending more and more time closer and closer to the ladder. If the progression is slow enough, the others will come to regard it as a normal part of their day. One day, she taps a single foot on the first rung—ever so briefly—and then removes it.

You see, no doubt, where this is going: other members of the environment absorb slow, incremental, and habitual changes more easily than quick ones. It is a point we have covered many times in this book and in many ways. So let's skip to the end. Fast-forward to the moment that our heroine, loitering near the top of the ladder in a way that the group has come to expect and allow, finally reaches up and grabs the bananas. Amid surprise, fear, and possibly a little hostile screeching, she rips apart the bunch, tosses a banana or two to each of her compatriots, and triumphantly begins to eat one. And then . . .

Nothing happens. Nothing bad happens, and nothing terribly exciting happens either. Viewed from outside, it's just a bunch of monkeys eating bananas.

Yet at that moment, life in the cage has permanently changed. It is different for everyone, and most especially, it is different for our heroine. She probably doesn't fully realize it. She may be reveling in the taste of her banana or in the appreciation of those around her. Perhaps she is looking forward to a few extra dollars in her paycheck, a promotion, or a plaque and a 20-dollar gift certificate to a local eatery as a thank-you from monkey management.

Most likely, she doesn't fully grasp what's really transpired. From her perspective, she just took the next incremental step toward a goal she'd been working toward for a long time. But consider the impact on everyone else: she's just taught them that one of their unquestioned assumptions about reality was wrong. The surprise removal of such an assumption leaves only new questions in the minds of the rest of the group: Was this always possible? Will it be possible again? What other opportunities have we ignored? Should we make new rules about this? Can any of us do this, or is the one who did it somehow special?

Our heroine, of course, doesn't have these questions, because her reality hasn't changed. To the others, the world has been disrupted, while to her, the world still makes sense. As a result, it becomes apparent to all the other monkeys that if anyone has answers to the questions plaguing them, she does. In fact, at some level, conscious or not, her peers begin to suspect that she may have answers not only to questions that worry them but also to questions they haven't thought about yet.

That, as you can imagine, is a lot of responsibility for a monkey. It's also a lot of responsibility for you.

The Advice Equation

How often are you asked for advice? How frequently do others ask permission to bounce something off you or "tap your brain" regarding a problem? How regularly does someone suggest that if you don't know the answer, you probably know who will? How often do you find yourself providing suggestions that people appreciate? The answers to these questions indicate how your work group regards the utility of your cultural patterns.

This issue is a bit tricky to discuss. For one thing, the English language doesn't have an exact word for it. The closest nouns are words like *status* and *reputation*. But *status* implies something about your level in the organizational hierarchy, and *reputation* can be used for anything from how socially desirable you are to how quickly you get things done. Neither of these is what we mean. In fact, both confuse the issue.

"Crystalline reputation" is not about formal organizational status, popularity, or speed of results, although it does have a cause-and-effect relationship to those issues. Often, as your crystalline reputation improves, your career will advance, your standing with peers will improve, and the pace at which you produce results will quicken. But what we're discussing here is a specific form of organizational wisdom that lies behind those issues: the way in which your colleagues regard the cultural patterns you demonstrate. It is the improvement in your crystalline reputation that precedes and produces those other improvements in your work life.

You began this book as a member of the culture surrounding you, following roughly the same precedents and probably producing roughly the same output as others in your crystalline network. As you first began to role-model new cultural patterns, you became a contributor to your workplace, bringing to it new ways of doing things and probably a little more effectiveness. But as you can see from Figure 7.1, your journey will not end there. With continued, consistent, habitual demonstration of your patterns of overtness and clarity, your crystalline reputation will improve. Over time, you will naturally come to play the role of advisor, as others begin to suspect that you have answers and try to seek them out. Finally, as your influence grows even more, your role as advisor will expand further to the role of definer of cultural trends. At that point, you will have a growing network of trusting relationships with others in influential positions, many of whom owe a small part of their success to your role-modeling.

Types of Advice

For now, let's start with your role as advisor. The better you get at role-modeling your new cultural precedents—being overt about your tasks and the tasks of others, and practicing clarity regarding your relationships with others—the better informed you'll be about

FIGURE 7.1 Corresponding increases in output capability and your perceived value to the group

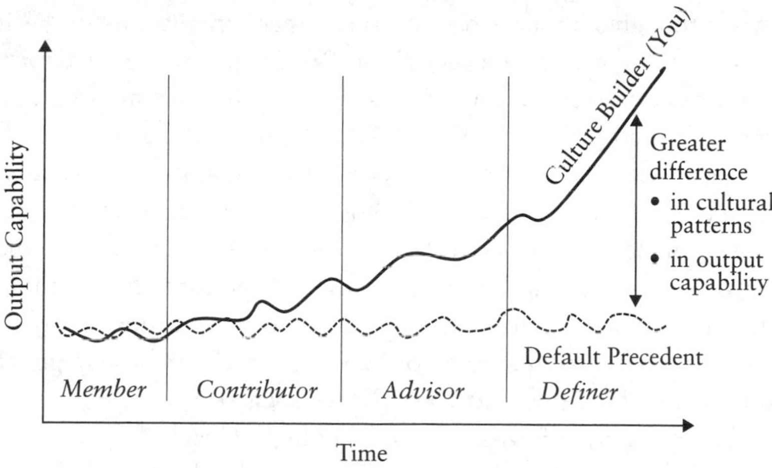

what is going on around you and the better informed others will be about your purpose and activity. As a result, your behavior will seem progressively more novel to those around you, and you will seem to produce outputs more easily. Like our fictitious monkey heroine, you probably won't feel much different—and you certainly won't be magically imbued with infinite wisdom. But those around you will begin, ever so slowly, to perceive you differently as they begin to glimpse the fact that you are successfully making work great.

That is your crystalline reputation, and the frequency with which others ask for your advice is an indicator of it. Of course, this is not to say that you should go around offering unsolicited advice! To do so would run counter to your goals. What you must do, however, is become skilled at giving advice when it is requested.

Solicitations for your advice come in three forms. First (and simplest) are information requests—such as "Where's the bathroom?" or "Who approves expense forms?" These requests can be handled quickly, with little investigation or reflection. They have little to do with your crystalline reputation; you will probably get some of them no matter where you are on the graph in Figure 7.1, and you certainly don't need this book to tell you how to respond.

Second are requests for feedback. These are usually people asking for your thoughts about a past or future performance, as in "What did you think of my presentation?" or "What tips do you have for me before I meet with this client?" These requests become more frequent in the contributor phase of Figure 7.1. The main thing to remember about feedback requests is to be attentive to timing. If your intent is to reinforce something positive, you should give the feedback just after the performance is completed. But if you intend to suggest a change, you should give your input just before the next performance. Although it requires a little more effort to have separate conversations at specific times, this type of timing is the only way to ensure that your positive feedback is encouraging and your change suggestions are usable. (See Chapter 4 for more information about giving feedback.)

The balance of this chapter is dedicated to the third type of advice requests, solicitations for situational advice. These requests, the real indicators of your migration to the advisor phase of Figure 7.1, are the most nebulous. They are often disguised as complaints or impossible problems. They're harder to identify as advice requests and require much more thought on your part as the advisor. However, they are also excellent chances to increase the reach and impact of your new cultural patterns.

Recognizing a Request for Situational Advice: "What" and "If"

The most important pieces of information regarding situational advice requests are "what" and "if." You must become skilled at determining both *what* a person is concerned about and *if* he or she is asking for your advice about it. This sounds so simple, but many people are frequently wrong about "what" and "if," or they forget to ask the questions entirely. If you make these mistakes, you miss opportunities to provide useful advice. You may also damage trust by making others suspect that you don't understand them or that you're trying inappropriately to force your views on them. Many interactions that end in frustration begin with misunderstood answers to "what" and "if."

Once in a while, a person will ask plainly and directly for your thoughts or ideas about a specific situation, and the "what" and "if" will both be built into the request: "I'm having a problem with a coworker, and I'd like to get your thoughts on the situation." More often, advice requests begin as problem statements or complaints: "I can't get Mary to do her weekly report, no matter how many times I ask her," or "There's no way one person can do all the work that's assigned to me." In cases like these, it's up to you to discover "what" and "if" for yourself.

It can be difficult to remember to do this. When you hear negative statements, your natural inclination is to end the complaining. You may attempt to do this by solving the problem quickly: "Tell Mary she could get fired for not writing her report," or "Make a list of your priorities and have your manager approve it." In other words, "Take this answer and leave me alone!" Or you may end the discomfort by exiting without engaging: "That's too bad. Excuse me, I have a meeting." Unfortunately, neither of these very human responses serves to build trust, provide useful solutions, or reinforce the importance of your cultural precedents.

That's why it's so important to stay focused on the answers to "what" and "if." You must help the other person fully develop his or her story and then ask specifically whether advice is desired.

Discovering "What"

Developing the story is as simple as seeking information. Your first response to a person's initial problem statement or complaint should be neither a suggestion nor an excuse to depart. Instead, say either, "Tell me more about that," or "And what else?" Make sure that your body language and intonation are interested and inquisitive, not accusatory or assertive. Invite the other person to have a seat, make eye contact, and become engaged. Don't check your watch or attempt to write an e-mail during your conversation! Your goal—your only goal—is to learn about the other person's situation, so that you can paint a clearer picture in your own mind of what's really going on. You need to be listening, and your body language needs to show it.

Notice that this approach is different than asking questions such as "Why is that a problem?" or "How long has this been happening?" The act of questioning is verbally aggressive: it puts the other person on the spot to provide answers, and it forces the conversation toward the topic of your question. Your goal, by contrast, is to put the other person at ease and allow him or her to direct the topic of the conversation to what is most important. Mary's lack of weekly reports may ultimately be due to a problem with Mary, a problem with the weekly reports, or a problem with Mary's manager, to name just a few possibilities. Asking "When was the last time Mary wrote a report?" may answer your most pressing inquiry, but it may push many more useful areas of exploration to the back burner.

Your goal is understanding, not analysis. Imagine that you're planning to produce a movie of the situation. As the producer, you're far more interested in the story line than in the outcome for any individual character. Listen carefully to what you hear so that you learn the details of the situation, the characters, and the conflicts involved. Three conversational techniques can be helpful in this regard:

- **Make open-ended requests for information.** Ideally, the person will talk—and you'll listen—until the whole story is disclosed. But the mechanics of conversation require that you respond with some frequency to show that you're still engaged and that you want to hear more. While you can't just keep parroting the phrase "Tell me more about that," you can—and should—continuously express interest in the other person's version of the situation until he or she is done. Remember the power of nonverbal cues and show the person you're listening. If you can't give the matter your full attention, ask for the person's permission to schedule the conversation a little later.
- **Clarify by tentatively rephrasing your understanding as you go.** The stronger your focus on trying to re-create the story, the more often you'll find yourself wishing for clarification about certain ele-

ments of it. Perhaps you don't fully understand the importance of Mary's weekly reports. Instead of asking a potentially leading question, offer your tentative understanding along with openness to clarification: "It sounds like the main purpose of the weekly reports is to update the other members of the group. Do I have that right, or is there more?"

- **Ask questions about your conversation, not about the story.** If the other person seems to be digressing, you can certainly check whether that's true: "Can you help me here? I don't want to lose you. We started off talking about Mary's progress, but we seem now to be deep in the topic of company accounting processes. Are we still on track?" This question is designed not to analyze the story but to check on the development of your understanding. At the same time, it communicates the importance you place on fully grasping what the person is telling you. Pay close attention to the answer. What seems like a digression to you may actually be the most important point: it may be the company accounting processes that are creating Mary's overload.

Your real goal is to have the other person agree that you understand his or her perspective of the situation. Summarizing what you've learned as the story draws to a close will help wrap up this part of your investigation: "So Mary has either failed to write her weekly summary report or turned it in late for the past seven weeks. You've tried addressing the issue with her privately, but she has been unwilling to discuss it. You've also tried restating your expectations with the whole group. Still, you have yet to see any change in Mary's behavior, her current report is two days late and counting, and you are growing ever more frustrated. Do I have that about right?" Again, speak tentatively and give the other person an opportunity to correct you. Try to capture both the facts and the emotions involved. This is your last chance to understand.

Discovering "If"

Next, you're ready to move to the question of "if" your advice is being solicited. This is as simple as asking, "Are you seeking my advice, or are you just sharing information?" Pose the question honestly, with no expectation. Either answer is fine! In this situation, anything that isn't an obvious "Yes, I want your advice," should be treated as a "no." Don't offer advice unless you're sure.

You may be wondering why you waited this long to ask the "if" question. Why not start by finding out if the person is looking for your advice, so you can avoid the long conversation if the answer is no? Imagine the two possible outcomes of this approach. If the person starts out asking for your advice, the conversation will follow the same pattern anyway. But if he or she starts out by declining your advice, then what do you do? Do you say, "Well, go ahead and tell me the story anyway," or do you tell the person to come back when he or she is ready for your advice? Neither of these awkward answers is particularly conducive to information transfer, trust building, or the demonstration of your new cultural precedents.

This person has approached you and wants to tell you the story. Your openness to it confirms one of his or her unstated assumptions—that you will listen. In the telling, the person will verbally process the information and, at the same time, build his or her level of trust and

Recognizing a Request for Advice ("What" and "If")

- Make open-ended requests for information.
- Seek clarity by offering interim summaries of what you believe to be the speaker's understanding.
- Ask questions about your conversation, not about the story.
- Obtain the other person's agreement that you understand his or her version of the story, including both the factual and the emotional content.
- Ask the other person directly whether he or she is seeking your advice.

comfort with you. At the end of the telling, he or she may have come to a better understanding of what's happened. He or she will also have developed more interest in your advice and more trust in you, because you now understand the situation. When you wait until the end of the story to ask if the person wants your advice, the answer is more likely to be "yes," and the person is more likely to be receptive of what you have to say.

If, at the end of the story, the person says "no," you've still built trust and mutual understanding and demonstrated your unwillingness to force your views on others. Simply say, "I'm glad I could be here to listen," and leave it at that. You may well find that after a little time, the person returns to ask for your advice.

Setting the Stage for Your Advice

What if the person does ask for your advice? Once you understand the situation and have been asked for advice, your job is to give the answer, right?

Perhaps not. Advice requests, often framed as complaints, represent the frustrations of others in attempting to get their work done, reach their goals, and/or experience some enjoyment in the process. When these frustrated people look to you for help, you have the opportunity to create or strengthen a mutually beneficial relationship. In doing so, you also further the reach of your new cultural patterns.

Use your patterns, and begin with overtness about purpose. Start by defining what you have to offer. For the first time since the interaction started, it's time for you to take a leadership role in the conversation and articulate the parameters of your interaction going forward. Four areas in particular deserve special attention:

- **Reiterate the advice request and explain what it entails.** Say, "You've asked me for my advice, so I'm going to try to put myself in your situation. This means I'll probably be asking you some specific questions about what you're facing. Please understand that this is not a quiz. There are no wrong answers. I just want to understand."

Be sure that both the tone and content of your questions stay consistent with this intention. Asking "What kept you from recognizing this as a problem sooner?" can communicate very different messages depending on the tone you use.

- **Define the kinds of advice you can give.** Say, "There are basically two kinds of advice I can offer you: things I see and things I would do. The things I see are aspects of the situation that seem important to me, based on my experience. The things I would do are actions I believe I'd take if I were in your shoes." As the discussion progresses, separate the two as you share your insights: "To me, the fact that Mary hasn't responded to your requests for timely reports is significant—that's something I see. Personally, I would treat this as a missed commitment on her part and begin a formal reprimand. That's what I would do." Even if your advisee isn't comfortable taking the action you suggest, he or she can still consider the issue you've identified.
- **Give permission to disregard your advice.** Say, "Remember that you have a better understanding of what's going on than I do, and you may also have a different approach. Just because I see something as important doesn't mean you have to agree. And just because I would do something a certain way doesn't mean you must. Whatever you decide won't change our relationship or make me less willing to give you advice in the future." Stay true to this promise, and never say, "I told you so," if someone returns with a tale of your advice going unheeded. It won't be necessary anyway—the lesson will already have been learned; indeed, it will probably be the reason for the return visit.
- **Remind the person of his or her own responsibility.** It never hurts to remind the other person that you're offering insights and ideas, but not directing him or her—and certainly not providing an excuse for otherwise inexcusable action. Say, "Don't interpret anything I say as the suggestion, direction, or permission to do something illegal, dangerous, or unethical. You're still responsible here. The final decision of what you do is up to you, because the consequences of your actions are entirely yours, and you understand your situation better than I do."

Setting the Stage for Advice

- Reiterate the request for advice and explain what it entails.
- Define the different kinds of advice you can give.
- Give the other person permission to disregard your advice.
- Remind the person of his or her own responsibility.

Obviously, you may choose different wording than what appears in these examples. Just be sure to address all four areas as you set the stage for discussion: You are the advisor, and the other person is the decider and the doer. By appropriately allocating these responsibilities, you will be better positioned to give pertinent, useful advice and less likely to be misinterpreted, misunderstood, or misquoted later.

Giving Your Advice

After your preparation and stage-setting, you are ready to start giving advice. So what, exactly, are you going to talk about?

One of the challenges of giving situational advice is that to a large extent, you can't prepare in advance. Requests often come up unexpectedly and spontaneously. Even with a model like the one in the last section, it's difficult to prepare for a conversation that may or may not be a request for advice about a topic that may or may not have ever come up before. In many ways, advising is an improvisational art.

Can improvisation be avoided? You could try to predict the other person's request, but you run the risk of being blinded by your expectations and misunderstanding the real need. You might also ask for time to think about things after you've heard the story and the request, an approach that has some merit—especially in highly complex, involved, or perilous situations. But things change. As you ponder, your advisee's situation develops further, and your understanding decreases. Besides, the phrase "Yes, I'm asking for your advice" is the opening of a door, and doors don't stay open forever. Small, useful insights offered at the moment of receptivity may have more impact than well-thought-out analyses presented days later.

After you've heard the request for advice and set the stage for giving it, it's best to quickly transition from understanding your advisee's situation to offering insights about it. To do so, you'll need an interpretive framework—some set of experiences or concepts that will help you efficiently make sense of what you've just heard.*

The Framework of Experience

The first and most common framework is personal experience. As you listen to another person's situation, you naturally seek similarities with your own. You hear of Mary's unwillingness to complete her regular reports, you observe the frustration it causes, and you naturally recall being frustrated when a member of your own staff wouldn't comply with reporting directives. Or perhaps you had an employee who wrote confusing status reports or a manager who set ill-defined expectations regarding your own reporting. Any of these experiences may occur to you and naturally become your first interpretive framework.

Personal experiences provide excellent starting points for understanding someone else's situation. They allow you to empathize, give you a context for asking questions, and provide the opportunity to share personal stories, which is a powerful form of advising. On the other hand, personal experiences are limited by your memories. You risk recalling only the most positive or—especially—most negative situations, and you risk "selective memory" of your own role. Worse, your experiences may be only peripherally related to your advisee's current situation. The looser the connection, the more of a stretch it is to find relevance in the story. Perhaps most significantly, you often

---

*This, by the way, is another good reason to seek to fully understand the situation before asking the other person if he or she is requesting your advice. Once you know for certain that you are expected to provide advice, your thoughts will naturally gravitate toward what you are going to say. If this happens too early in your colleague's disclosure of his or her situation, it is far too easy to miss critical details of the situation because you are distracted by the planning of your responses.

remember personal experiences in the context of an intense lesson, a kind of "note to self": your bad manager didn't set firm expectations about your regular reports, and it caused a huge problem. The moral of *your* story is that managers should always be specific about reporting requirements. That's a good lesson for you, but it may have nothing to do with your advisee's problem with Mary.

You can—and no doubt will—use your experience as one framework for understanding other people's situations. It is important, however, to remember that it has limits.

The Framework of Models

Models, or the concrete representation of abstract ideas, are everywhere. They come at every level of specificity, from how to conceptualize a corporate revenue stream to how to wire a light switch. The right model can be a powerful advisory tool: if you can take another person's situation, help analyze it using a relevant model, and together draw conclusions from the results, you have the platform for giving some truly outstanding advice. If, during the process, you're also able to draw parallels between the conclusions the model suggests and your personal experiences, your advice will be that much more powerful and memorable.

Advising with models also has its own set of challenges. For one thing, your analysis and conclusions are only as relevant as the model you choose. The sheer number of available models can be overwhelming, and it's easy to inadvertently pick one because of its familiarity or ease of use rather than its appropriateness to the situation. As Abraham Maslow said, "When the only tool you have is a hammer, it is tempting to treat everything as if it were a nail."

Perhaps more importantly, if the model is too complex or abstract, or if your advisee is resistant to it for some reason, you'll find yourself derailed, caught in a conversation about the model instead of the situation. If you're not able to provide some linkage from the model back to your personal experience (a story or example to support its practicality), then you'll have eliminated the personal connection that is the very reason your advisee sought you in the first place. When this happens, your advice begins to seem impersonal and detached.

As you can see, to give truly outstanding situational advice, you need to combine personal experience with the framework of a model and offer your advisee insights and suggestions that make use of both.

Culture-Driven Advice: The Best of Both Worlds

The good news is that at this point in your development as a cultural crystal builder, you already have a perfect set of practical models and a body of related experience to use as an advisor. Your models are designed to enhance workplace performance and have a built-in set of questions to help you hone in on the most important issues of the moment. You've practiced using them yourself, so they are integrated with your personal experiences and allow you to blend theoretical suggestions with practical examples. Your models are targeted yet flexible, so they almost always lead to useful discussion and action. Best of all, you probably have them memorized by now.

These models are the cultural patterns you've been demonstrating: your practices of overtness about task and clarity about relationship. The use of your new cultural patterns as an advisory framework should strike you as being, if nothing else, extremely logical. These patterns of workplace activity have led you to receive more requests for advice in the first place. Why not use them as part of your response? After all, at a conceptual level, advice seekers who perceive you moving toward the right of the graph in Figure 7.1 are really asking you to explain what you're doing differently. The specific complaint or issue they bring up is the context for having the conversation, a particular excuse to ask about the general pattern. By incorporating the general pattern in your response, you help them with the specific issue while still having a broader discussion and helping them become that much more self-sufficient for the next similar issue that arises.

Using your new cultural precedents as an advisory framework is actually quite straightforward. After your advice has been requested, you can investigate any aspect of overtness or clarity as part of your exploration. If you're unsure where to begin, the best approach is to step through all of the components in the order in which you first learned them. In other words, begin with purpose.

Tables 7.1 and 7.2 provide examples of the kinds of issues you can explore about each type of overtness and clarity, as well as the answers you can expect. Much of the detail is omitted in these summaries. They are not intended to replace the expertise you've developed in being overt about tasks and seeking clarity about relationships, and they shouldn't be used as handouts for your advisee. Rather, they are intended as job aids to help guide you in applying your expertise.

As you review the tables, notice the slight but important difference between them. Table 7.1 outlines the advice process when the issue has to do with overtness about task. In these cases, your advisee may be having trouble with his or her own tasks or may be having trouble getting someone else to do something. The table allows for this difference between advisee and performer. Table 7.2, on the other hand, focuses on issues of relationship. In these cases, the focus should stay on the advisee. When you're advising someone about his or her relationship with another person, it is neither practical nor useful to give suggestions to the absent party. Instead, keep your suggestions focused on what your advisee might do differently him- or herself.

Using these tables will help you narrow down your discussion to a specific area. Remember to do this! Your goal is to address what you believe to be the most important issue. After all, none of us can

Quick Video: Improving Output

Visit www.MakeWorkGreat.com for a short video segment about how to advise others using the six forms of overtness about task. This is also an easy bit of information to share if you're trying to describe the contents of this chapter to a trusted friend or colleague.

TABLE 7.1 Using Overtness About Task as an Advisory Framework

	Overtness About Task Area of Exploration (advisee/performer)*	Answer Indicating This Area Is Not an Issue	Answer Indicating This Area May Be an Issue	Suggestions
PURPOSE	(1) Can the advisee exactly state the output required? (2) Can the performer exactly state the output required?	(1) The advisee states the output requirement for the task (what, by when). (2) The performer has explained the output requirement, in his/her own words, to the advisee.	The advisee or performer has an incomplete or unclear understanding of the output requirement.	Work with the advisee on how to craft a summary outputs statement as it applies to this task. Encourage the advisee to work with the performer for mutual understanding and/or agreement regarding the output requirement.
IMPACT	(1) Does the advisee fully understand the impact or importance of the task? (2) Does the performer fully understand the impact or importance of the task?	(1) The advisee can fully articulate the benefit of the task to the organization. (2) The advisee and performer have discussed the impact and importance of the work.	The advisee or performer is unable to articulate the impact of the work or is unclear or conflicted as to whether the completion of the work would have a beneficial effect on the organization.	Work with the advisee to define the impact, check for unintended adverse effects, and discuss these issues with the performer.

INCENTIVES	(1) Can the advisee state the positive consequences of the output to the performer? (2) Would the performer agree with those positive consequences?	(1) The advisee fully understands the positive and adverse consequences to the performer that are associated with the output required. (2) The performer agrees with these consequences and has stated this to the advisee.	The advisee and/or performer is unable to articulate why the performer would be inclined to perform the task, other than simple rationales such as "it's required."	Work with the advisee to more fully define the positive and negative consequences of the output to the performer and to share them with the performer to check for agreement.
PROGRESS	(1) Does the advisee know whether the performer is using a visibility system to track progress and, if so, what it is? (2) Is the performer's progress apparent to himself/herself using a simple visibility system hourly or daily?	(1) The advisee is aware of the existence of a visibility system, or the performer usually knows whether or not he/she is making progress without outside advice. (2) The performer can explain how he/she tracks his/her progress on an hourly or daily basis.	There is a sense from either the advisee or the performer that the performer is "spinning his/her wheels" and working without a clear sense of progress or advancement.	Explain the purpose of visibility systems and help the advisee define or refine his/her own monitoring methods so he/she can coach the performer to do the same.

(continued)

	Overtness About Task Area of Exploration (advisee/performer)*	Answer Indicating This Area Is Not an Issue	Answer Indicating That This Area May Be an Issue	Suggestions
RESOURCES	(1) Does the advisee understand the resources required by the performer to complete the task and whether the performer has access to those resources? (2) Does the performer understand what those resources are? Does he/she have access to those resources?	(1) The advisee may or may not have a full recollection of all the resources required but can explain the method in place for the performer to access resources as he/she needs them. (2) The performer can articulate the resources needed for the task and explain how he or she can access them easily.	(1) The advisee or performer doesn't appear to have fully considered the resources needed. (2) The performer can't access the resources needed due to scarcity or complex approval processes.	Work with the advisee to help the performer build a complete resources list and to support the performer in finding ways to make necessary resources available or change the scope of the task accordingly.
CAPABILITY	(1) Does the advisee know whether the performer has the proper skills to complete the task? (2) Has the performer indicated that there is or is not any skill gap?	(1) The advisee can explain the key hard and soft skills required for the task and the performer's suitability. (2) The performer has the ability to do the task if all other areas of overtness have been answered in the affirmative.	The performer may not possess certain technical or nontechnical skills that seem important to the task, or the advisee or performer may not have a clear understanding of what skills are required.	Work with the advisee to formulate definitions of the skills required and to carefully and nonjudgmentally help the performer develop them.

**Note: If the advisee (the person speaking with you) is also the performer (the person doing the task), the two roles collapse into one.*

TABLE 7.2 Using Clarity Within Relationship as an Advisory Framework

	Clarity About Relationship Area of Exploration	Answer Indicating This Area Is Not an Issue	Answer Indicating This Area May Be an Issue	Suggestions
CLARITY OF QUESTION	What information is needed from the other person? Which areas of overtness are most important? What questions must be asked and answered? What information is extraneous or unnecessary?	The advisee can articulate the need for information exchange between himself/herself and the other(s) involved and discuss the clarifications or areas of overtness that are most pertinent to the discussion.	The advisee has a vague or poorly defined sense of what he/she is seeking from the other person.	Help the advisee to define the overtness, information, and action he/she needs from the other person and to discuss those needs during their next interaction. (See Table 7.1 to define areas of overtness.)
CLARITY OF APPROACH	How does the other person process information? What are the best strategies for interacting with him/her? What pressures does he/she face? How is the advisee using this knowledge to plan the interaction?	The advisee understands how best to communicate with the other person, including approaches that have worked well or poorly in the past. The advisee incorporates this information into his/her plan for the next interaction.	The advisee uses his/her "default approach" rather than tuning it to the other person's needs. The advisee seems unaware of or disinterested in the other person's perspective.	Work with the advisee to understand the position and pressures of the other person. Use the interactive troubleshooting model to consider possible information, situation, interpretation, approach, and beliefs on both sides. (See Fig. 6.3 for a model.)

(continued)

Clarity About Relationship Area of Exploration		Answer Indicating This Area Is Not an Issue	Answer Indicating This Area May Be an Issue	Suggestions
CLARITY OF THE NEED FOR AGREEMENT	What must the two people agree on? In what areas might it be more appropriate for the advisee and the other person to agree to disagree?	The advisee can clearly articulate the agreement needed and is comfortable sustaining disagreements in related but noncritical areas.	The advisee tries to obtain across-the-board agreement with the other person, inadvertently seeking to create a convert rather than solve a specific problem.	Help the advisee hone in on exactly what agreement is necessary, and offer to agree to disagree as an alternative in the other areas.

handle too much information at once. Step through each row of the tables, one at a time, until you hit on the first issue; stop there. If you continue—if your advice is an overwhelming set of suggestions or ideas—it will most likely be ignored. Focus carefully and help your advisee consider some manageable changes that are likely to help. You can always return to the "next important thing" later, after the first important thing has been addressed.

An Emerging Role

Your migration from cultural contributor to cultural advisor will probably be more gradual than the earlier story of our fictitious monkey heroine might imply. This is good news for you, because advising is a skill that improves with practice and experience. Like every other transition discussed in this book, it is to your benefit to make the change slowly and manageably. The more advice you give and the more practice you have yourself, the deeper the base of knowledge and experience from which you can draw.

On the other hand, you should never feel disqualified by a self-perceived lack of knowledge. If you're practicing overtness and clarity, those around you already know what you're doing. When they seek your counsel, it's because they believe you have something to offer based on what they've seen of you already. Your only responsibility is to do your best to discover that something and offer it.

Giving Culture-Driven Advice

- Explore the other person's situation in terms of overtness about task and clarity about relationship.
- As you discover issues, limit yourself to one (or at most, two) areas of overtness and clarity.
- If possible, relate the issues you're discussing to your own experience and share a personal story.

Whatever you do, don't feel as though you need to force this. As with everything else we've discussed, the emergence of advisees and your corresponding comfort level with the role of advisor will happen naturally, just as your crystal grows organically. This may sound all too familiar, but stay true to your good habits and the rest will take care of itself.

EXERCISES

1. Consider how frequently others ask for your advice and what types of advice they solicit. Has the frequency changed since you began building your new culture? Have you noticed a change in the number of requests for your feedback or situational advice, as opposed to informational requests? Keep an awareness of this frequency to monitor for changes in the future.

2. The next time someone comes to you with a complaint, treat it as a request for situational advice and follow the suggestions in this chapter. Begin by establishing the answers to "what" and "if"—that is, learn as much as you can about the situation, then ask the person directly whether he or she is seeking your advice. If your advice is indeed being sought, set the stage carefully by explaining what you have to offer, and then use your new cultural patterns as models for the suggestions you make.

8 Mobilizing Groups

Imagine being given three wooden blocks—the same simple building blocks that have entertained toddlers for decades—along with a request: "Please build a structure optimized for height and stability." This isn't a complex task, and it won't take long. Most likely, you will take little time to seek outside input. You'll stack your blocks and be done with it.

Suppose that on seeing your result, your requester is pleased and returns with about 20 multicolored blocks of various sizes and shapes, along with a slightly modified task: "Please build a structure that is optimized for height, stability, and aesthetic appeal." This time, you might be inclined to seek some advice. Perhaps you will ask the requester for a bit more clarity regarding the meaning of "aesthetic appeal." Perhaps you'll turn to a nearby colleague to ask if he or she has ever been given this assignment. Ultimately, you will do the work yourself, but it might be wise to seek a little guidance first, as you now have both more options and more constraints.

Now imagine that your block-bearing requester is a wealthy and extremely eccentric property developer. Impressed by your performance on these building-block exercises, he decides to put you in charge of his next development project, a high-rise building in a heavily populated metropolitan area. He makes you an employment offer you can't refuse, and within minutes, you find yourself responsible for a capital construction project. Your options—and your constraints—have increased exponentially. Now what?

Probably most apparent is what you don't do: you don't just "ask around" or "start building"! As Figure 8.1 shows, your assignment has jumped in complexity and now requires more planning and collaboration. It's no longer possible to do it alone, nor will a little advice from a nearby colleague suffice. What you need is a team of experts to assist you with a plan.

This story may sound far-fetched, but its point is extremely relevant. We work with groups of people not because it's easy or fun or because "teamwork" is an idealistic notion. We do it because it's required. To successfully navigate the complexity of our early information age workplace and produce output from the crystalline network, we convene groups of experts to bring their expertise together. To succeed, these experts must find ways to reconcile and integrate the requirements and constraints they understand as individuals

FIGURE 8.1 Corresponding increase between the need for advice/collaboration and the complexity of an assignment

Increasing complexity of assignment →

"Optimize for height and stability"

Performer
- Acts quickly
- Seeks no counsel
- Works individually

"Optimize for height, stability, and aesthetic appeal"

Performer
- Reflects, then acts
- Seeks advice
- Works independently

"Optimize for safety, footprint, regulations, usability, aesthetic appeal, etc."

Performer
- Plans extensively
- Engages experts
- Works collaboratively

with the requirements and constraints understood by the rest of the group.

One person acting alone can't even procure the permits required to build a skyscraper, much less design or construct the actual building. And it doesn't matter whether you're building a skyscraper, redesigning a payroll system, manufacturing the next generation of smart phone, or designing an optimal software user interface. Group work is required in the production of complex results in the same way that flour, water, and yeast are required in the production of leavened bread.

Not coincidentally, group work is also essential to the production of the change you're making to your workplace culture. Could there be a more complex result to pursue? Sooner or later, as a natural outcome of your role as culture builder, you'll be required to go beyond advising individuals and move into the realm of influencing and directing groups of people. This can't be helped! As your crystal grows, you'll be accomplishing more, taking on more complex assignments, and receiving more requests for advice.

Groups: Your Next Frontier

Anytime you're in a conversation with more than one other person, you're engaged in a group setting. Your need to understand and handle group work well is a purely practical requirement for your continued success. Ideally, the groups with which you're involved will also begin to see and adopt the "group versions" of your new cultural patterns. When they do, you'll begin to see serious change in the world around you. You'll also experience what research has shown to be the good news about learning and problem solving in groups: if allowed sufficient time and equipped with proper interactive processes, groups outperform even their most capable individual members and generate ideas and solutions that go beyond what each member brings to the table singularly.[1] Good group work is essential in the crystalline network!

In any event, you must keep your eye on what happens in groups, because you're in the business of role-modeling your new precedents of behavior at all times. As the demonstrator of new patterns, you're always on stage, and never is that more true than in a group setting. There, the actions you take and the patterns of behavior you use are on display for everyone to see. If you're actually leading the group, your role presents an even greater opportunity—and even greater risk—because you're involving everyone in your personal solution to the optimization question of the critical ratio of output versus stress. When you get it right and demonstrate how your cultural patterns produce positive outcomes with minimal stress, you further both your work objectives and your culture-building objectives. When you get it wrong and create confusion, stress, or agitation, you harm your credibility, your output, and the growth of your cultural crystal.

This means you must begin to interact with and influence groups of people working together. Being a one-on-one advisor is not enough; you must learn to make groups great too.

Why People Gather

At this point in the book, you shouldn't be surprised that you begin, yet again, with purpose. In the context of group work, this means that you must start by asking for overtness about the purpose of the group's coming together. Luckily, this is a particularly easy place to start, because at the highest level, all group work can be defined by one or both of two basic purposes: to inform or to solve.

When people come together for the dissemination of new information, the reinforcement of existing facts or policies, or the one-way transmission of assignments, the purpose is to inform. Quarterly earnings summaries, policy change announcement meetings, and action huddles in which work orders are handed out are ostensibly held for this purpose. Such meetings use a one-way transmission of factual information, as shown on the left side of Figure 8.2. It's important to realize, however, that the type of information being transferred need not be the overt, factual sort of data we visualize when we think about policy updates or marching orders. Groups exchange a second type of information that is equally important but much harder to rec-

FIGURE 8.2 Information transfer (left) versus solution discussion (right)

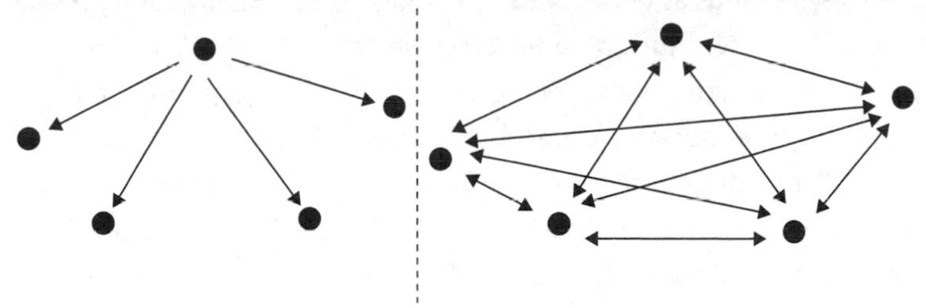

ognize: information about status or power. Underlying what is said in many information-sharing gatherings is the unspoken reinforcement of the roles and hierarchy of the organization, often called *politics*. Who makes the presentation may be as important as what information is presented. When a manager assigns and employees act, the interchange subtly reinforces the hierarchy between them. Similarly, the chairman of the board always opens the annual board meeting. These cues are subtle, but they are often at least as relevant to the purpose of the meeting as the content of the actual discussions.

Of course, in many cases, it's not enough simply to inform. The reality of the crystalline network is that not only do groups pass along information, but they solve problems and make decisions. In the new information age, the expression "many hands make light work" might well be replaced with "many *minds* make light work." When a group gathers for the purpose of coming to a conclusion, making a recommendation, taking action, deciding how to allocate limited resources, or crafting a response to an urgent problem, the dynamics of the situation are quite different than those of sharing information, as shown on the right side of Figure 8.2. In these cases, the goal is to solve a problem or answer a question. Whether it's the one-time, ad hoc gathering of a task force faced with the quick resolution of a crisis, or the monthly managers' meeting to make routine decisions about resource allocation, many group encounters focus on resolution of specific questions or issues.

Two Types of Meetings

Andy Grove, founder and former president of Intel Corporation, listed effective meetings as being among the key factors in any company's managerial success, including his own. He defined two specific types of group gatherings: "process-oriented" meetings designed to share information and expertise on a regular basis, and "mission-oriented" meetings designed to fulfill a specific mission and then disband.[2] In a broader analysis of effective group gatherings, William Daniels extended this distinction, defining the purpose of regular management meetings as the exercise of the organization's formal authority in the allocation of resources, and limiting the purpose of ad hoc task forces to making recommendations for solving specific problems.[3] The commonalities in these and related analyses of group effectiveness are the basis for the distinction in meeting types presented here.

The question about the broad purpose of the gathering—to inform, solve, or both—comes first, because it carries implications about everything else involving the meeting, including membership, content, and process. Information transfer is an exercise in one-way communication: the same factual or hierarchical information is put on display for everyone to see at once. As a result, the audience can be as small or as large as desired. The primary considerations regarding the factual information are issues like clarity of presentation and timeliness and accuracy of information. The primary considerations regarding the hierarchical information are issues such as speaker selection, order, ceremony, and timing.

Solution-type discussions, on the other hand, require a different sort of construction. The membership issues that matter most are whether you have the right experts present for the task at hand and whether the number of people involved allows for the kind of discussion and problem solving needed. An 18-person board of directors can ratify a proposal, but good luck getting all of the members to cre-

Quick Video: Meeting Types—Information vs. Solution

Visit www.MakeWorkGreat.com for a short video segment about how to recognize and utilize the two types of meetings. This is also an easy bit of information to share if you're trying to describe the contents of this chapter to a trusted friend or colleague.

ate one together! If you've ever experienced the pain of a group of a dozen or more people trying to come to a conclusion about a problem, you know that as the number of participants exceeds seven or eight, it becomes progressively more difficult for people to be heard, much less understand each other and come to a real agreement.

Many meetings are created, intentionally or accidentally, with the dual purposes of informing and problem solving. Perhaps a group of coworkers at a weekly staff update takes a few minutes to answer a policy question before moving forward. Maybe the financial subcommittee of the board of directors steps away from an all-day board retreat during lunch to come up with some recommendations to share with the group in the afternoon. Combinations like these can lead to useful, productive output, or they can lead to confusion, agitation, and delays.

From your perspective as a culture builder, the difference between success and failure lies—as always—in overtness and clarity. In the context of meetings, this means the plain and correct definition of the meeting's logistics, attendance, content, and timing. While it may be impossible to bring all of the facets of the meeting into the open (influencing group politics, for example, is far beyond the scope of this book), the more you can use your own role-modeling to help a group become more purpose-driven in its function, the better off you and the rest of the participants will be.

The Meeting Specification: Beyond "Agenda"

It may surprise you that this book, with its complex and novel topic, would address such a seemingly basic issue as writing down the logistics of a meeting. We all know that meetings need agendas and invitations, don't we? But please resist the temptation to skip reading this section on the grounds that you already know what it contains. A quick survey of the meeting practices in most organizations—even those touted as having highly effective meetings—regularly turns up the same result: meetings are a consistent source of frustration, inefficiency, stress, and waste. In the crystalline workplace, group interactions are absolutely necessary, yet in some organizations, the word *meetings* has a connotation bordering on the obscene. Meetings are the bane of existence for executives, managers, and individual contributors alike. Much of the frustration—issues like "Why am I here?" "What are we doing?" "We're going in circles," and "No one's prepared"—can be traced back to the absence of comprehensive definitions or specifications for the gathering.

As a culture builder whose reach is increasing, you'll need to become comfortable with the use of meeting specifications within your own sphere of influence. It's not enough to simply list some topics of discussion and call it an agenda. A specification is far more comprehensive. The good news is that, like many of the concepts in this book, the construction of a meeting specification is simple in principle. It doesn't require advanced training or skills. All you need is the disciplined investment of sufficient time, time spent getting very specific about the purpose, objective, attendance, roles, responsibilities, and flow of the meeting.

Constructing the Specification

Having addressed the highest-level purpose of the meeting (to inform, solve, or both), your second step is to become more specific regarding the meeting's objective. You should write this as a short, one- or two-sentence statement of the overall goal for the gathering. The objective answers the question of "why" you're asking participants to come together. With your objective in place, you can create an attendee list to identify required participants, optional participants, and interested nonparticipants. Individual participants should also be assigned specific roles, such as chair, note taker, and time monitor, to help keep the meeting moving and keep everyone engaged.

After the participant list and roles, you need to address the simple logistical issues of timing and connection method. The latter may include both physical location and technical connection instructions, depending on whether the gathering is in person or between attendees in physically remote locations.

The combination of your objective, participant list, roles, and logistics becomes the basis for defining what will actually happen during the meeting. This "flow" is the largest part of the meeting specification and often takes the longest to construct. It resembles what might traditionally be referred to as an "agenda," because it articulates the topics of discussion. But it also goes further. It's not enough to merely make a laundry list of discussion items or speaker names. To use everyone's time most productively, you must define the actual flow of time, as if you were scripting a screenplay. You define each item that appears in the flow in terms of how long you expect it to last, who will lead that portion or be responsible for making sure it happens correctly, what content will be addressed, what the format will be, and—perhaps most important—what the expected outcome or purpose of that item is. Defining the flow is much like defining a sequence of minimeetings, each with its own objective.

Figure 8.3 shows an example of a meeting specification for a task force. The physical layout may vary, but all of the necessary elements are included in this example, which can be used as a meeting specification template for any type of gathering. If constructed correctly,

Quick Video: Turbocharge Your Meetings

Visit www.MakeWorkGreat.com for a short video segment about how to add expected outcomes to well-crafted meeting plans. This is also an easy bit of information to share if you're trying to describe the contents of this chapter to a trusted friend or colleague.

FIGURE 8.3 Sample meeting specification, including meeting logistics, roles, objective, and flow

FINANCIAL SUBCOMMITTEE TASK FORCE KICKOFF

OBJECTIVE: Develop recommended solutions to counteract current revenue reduction trend for presentation to/ratification by board of directors at their November meeting (on 11/25/10)

LOCATION: 5–6 attendees present in facility boardroom; Tom and Maria to call in remotely by dialing (555)123-4567

DATE: October 6, 2010

TIME: 9:00 A.M.–10:30 A.M. (Tom, Maria, and room projector on shared file service)

REQUIRED PARTICIPANTS: Paula (chair), Sue (note taker), Guy (time monitor), Tom (participation monitor), Maria, Larry, Bobby

OPTIONAL PARTICIPANT: Phil

INTERESTED NONATTENDEES (CC LIST): Abe, Lynne, Chelsea, Hal

Time	What	Who	Format	Expected Outcome
9:00–9:10	Call to order, define purpose and history	Paula	Presentation	Make everyone clear on our purpose; review flow of time and adjust if needed.
9:10–9:20	Introductions	Paula/all	Everyone introduces themselves, their role, time with company, and 1 concern (1 min. each).	Everyone learns who's here and what the group's major concerns are.

9:20–9:35	Budget presentation	Larry	Presentation with Q&A; start capture list for open questions.	Everyone understands the current state of the budget and its 3-year history.
9:35–9:45	Other data needed	Sue/all	Discussion: What other information do we need?	We list questions to be answered for the next meeting.
9:45–9:50	Telephone check	Paula	Quick query to telephone attendees	We ensure that remote participants are heard.
9:50–10:05	Brainstorm areas for consideration	Maria/all	Open brainstorming of possible areas of exploration	Consider all ideas; Maria will capture in real time for an on-screen display.
10:05–10:15	Choose top areas	Maria/all	Combination and prioritization discussion based on brainstorm list	Team agrees on 3–4 areas for initial investigation and assigns investigators.
10:15–10:20	Next meeting	Paula/all	Review proposed agenda for meeting 2 and discuss timing	Team agrees on timing and agenda for meeting 2.
10:20–10:25	Last thoughts and adjournment	Paula/all	Open call for ideas; final comments by Paula	We close the meeting.
Agenda to be published 36 hours in advance (Paula); notes to be published within 24 hours of meeting (Sue).				

a meeting specification like this one applies all of your new cultural patterns to the context of effective group work.

Notice that in terms of overtness about task, this entire template comes into play:

- The well-defined meeting objective represents overtness about *purpose* regarding the meeting and its components. Also, the assignment of specific roles to individual attendees—who will chair, monitor the progress of the meeting flow, take notes, ensure everyone stays engaged, and so on—gives those participants another overt expectation for what they'll do with their time in the session.
- The set of expected outcomes for each agenda item supports overtness about *impact*, or what will result from each part of the meeting. If the agenda is well constructed, the relationship between those impacts and the overall goal of the meeting should be apparent to everyone in attendance.
- Listing that overall goal also supports overtness about *incentive* for the attendees. It articulates the exact reason for the gathering, so individuals can find ways to relate that purpose to their own set of incentives.
- The entire meeting flow section is a visibility system for the meeting's *progress*, because it allows everyone, especially the meeting's leader, to see at a glance whether the meeting is on track. To make it truly useful, the schedule must be visible to all attendees at all times, not just at the meeting's start. In face-to-face settings, handouts are a good option; if some or all attendees are remote, e-mail or a shared file service may be used.
- The list of who will attend and who owns each item on the agenda is a way of being overt about the *resources* required for the meeting. Defining the meeting venue and agenda also highlights any other resources needed, such as supplies or technology.
- Listing an item owner for each agenda item is also a way of being overt about *capability* requirements; each responsible party knows in advance what he or she needs to bring to the table for the

meeting. If Larry doesn't already have the skills and/or knowledge to deliver the budget summary presentation, he needs to find them or renegotiate his commitment with Paula, the meeting's *leader.*

Notice also that in terms of clarity regarding relationships, the completeness of the meeting flow is the key:

- The definition of each item in the meeting flow provides clarity about the *question*, defining exactly what will be discussed and explored during each time segment.
- The definition of format provides clarity about the *approach*, so attendees know in advance what type of activity, discussion, or presentation to expect.
- The expected outcome of each item gives clarity about the *need for agreement*, if there is such a need. It is especially important in group settings to define the need for agreement and the process for obtaining agreement in advance of the first conflict; this way it becomes a boundary condition and not a point of contention.

Structured Flexibility

Of course, none of this is to say that a meeting specification, once written, can't be adjusted. To stay with the example in Figure 8.3, imagine that a question arises in Larry's budget presentation that grabs the group's attention. As the end of his allotted time approaches, the group is engaged in a seemingly important conversation that appears as though it will require at least another 15 minutes to resolve itself.

Quick Video: Group Decision Making That Works

Visit www.MakeWorkGreat.com for a short video segment about how to define the process for agreement in group settings. This is also an easy bit of information to share if you're trying to describe the contents of this chapter to a trusted friend or colleague.

Writing a Meeting Specification

1. Define the meeting's purpose: to inform, solve, or both.
2. Write a one- or two-sentence objective for the gathering.
3. Define mandatory and optional attendees and their roles.
4. Define the logistics for attendance and/or remote connection.
5. Write a meeting flow section that gives each meeting item's time, owner, format, and expected outcome.

As the meeting leader, should Paula allow the departure from the flow or stop the conversation and make a note to include it as part of a future meeting?

The answer depends on the importance of the newly introduced topic relative to the overarching goals of the meeting. The decision could go either way. The value of the meeting specification is that it forces the decision to be an overt one. Someone—the leader, the flow monitor, or another attendee—should speak up, noting that continued conversation about the new topic will not leave sufficient time for the other items. Perhaps each team member will be asked to quickly give his or her opinion regarding the relative importance of each. Then Paula can decide whether to change the plan or stick with the original one and return to the new topic later.

If the plan is changed, the change is overt. Perhaps it would make sense in this case to move the "Choose top areas" item to the beginning of the next meeting—or to conduct an e-mail poll for that purpose between meetings—in order to free time for this new and important discussion. The specific details are far less important than the fact that the entire group stays on the same page with respect to what's going on in the meeting.

Group Memory: Consistency and Follow-Through

One major by-product of using well-formed meeting specifications is that you will need better tracking in four specific areas. Like the meeting specification, you need to employ these lists in such a way that they're constantly visible to all attendees—either posted on the wall during face-to-face gatherings or made available electronically during virtual meetings.

- Decisions made and/or key points discussed are captured in what are often called the *meeting minutes*. The format of this list can vary widely depending on the meeting's purpose and the attendees' needs. The important point to remember is that, when a key conclusion is reached, it should immediately be written down for everyone to see and endorse as part of the meeting's permanent record. This minimizes the otherwise-common problem of individuals later claiming they either don't remember or don't agree with certain decisions or facts.
- Individual actions to be taken—sometimes also called *action items* (AIs) or *action requirements* (ARs)—are the commitments made by meeting participants to do something for the group: "Bobby will ask our manager if he'd like to receive the notes from our meeting and let Sue know by Tuesday," or "Larry will bring a chart of our annual expenditures to our follow-up meeting next week." Such a list ensures accountability for output and deadlines at the individual level, because it's visible to everyone and reviewed on a regular basis.
- Future discussion items, sometimes called an *agenda horizon*, often arise in situations like the financial subcommittee example we've been using. Real-time adjustments to the current meeting's schedule, new issues that need attention, or key milestones related to external factors (such as the last subcommittee meeting before the board meeting) all make it necessary to plan items for future meeting flows in advance.
- Topics of later interest—sometimes called *bin items* or *parking lot issues*—are similar to future discussion items except they don't warrant scheduling actual meeting time. They are often "good points" that are off-topic at the moment but may arise again later or can be handled outside the meeting. By capturing them on a list of future concerns and then periodically reviewing that list with the group, the

leader or facilitator builds the team's confidence that these details are not forgotten. This relieves the participants who raised the concerns from feeling that they have to repeat themselves in order to be heard.

Making these four lists constantly visible to all attendees at all times—an approach often called *group memory*—ensures that everyone stays on the same page with respect to current and past discussions. At the same time, the content of these lists infuses the meeting with a sense of consistency and follow-through. This should come as no surprise, considering that the lists are consistent with your new cultural precedents; they're basically a visibility system that supports overtness about purpose.

Pay Now or Pay Later

Obviously, all of this planning takes time. The writing of a meeting specification, for example, forces you to slow down and think carefully about what will happen, how long it will take, who will participate, and what will be accomplished. Doing so raises questions you must answer, inspires new ideas you should address, and sometimes leads to rethinking assumptions about your best approach and/or membership. In the process of writing the specification, you must often stop several times to seek answers to related questions and redefine your own understanding of what will happen. This requires disciplined effort.

As a rule of thumb, if you're responsible for defining the meeting (whether you're the chairperson or his or her delegate), you should spend at least one hour in preparation for every hour the meeting will last. In reality, this guideline will vary depending on the experience levels of those involved and the complexity of the task at hand. But the point is an important one: a one-hour meeting with eight attendees uses as much manpower as a full day of labor for one person. A series of five such meetings is equivalent to one employee's workweek. Preparation is critical.

This seems so obvious. You wouldn't expect an employee at any level to spend a week of work with no plan, no goals, no objectives, and no specific intention for his or her time. "We perform as we rehearse" is a general principle in the theater that applies equally here. Yet too often we're happy to hold one or more meetings in which we more or less decide to figure things out on the fly. The results are predictably negative, with agitation, confusion, boredom, and conflict becoming the norms.

Think of it this way: if one hour of preparation for a meeting of eight people saves just 10 minutes of meeting time, it has a hard return on investment of 33 percent; 60 minutes invested saves 80 minutes of manpower. The value only grows if there are more people in the meeting or if more time is saved. And such a simple calculation doesn't even take into account important benefits such as the value of the other work that gets done in the saved time; the value of reaching a solution sooner; or the value of demonstrating to others through positive experience that meetings are useful, productive, and necessary in the new crystalline workplace.

If you intend to be a culture builder, it always pays to prepare for group interactions. It is far cheaper to pay now than later.

Making the Change

How do you incorporate this type of discipline into your meetings? For one thing, whenever you're in charge of bringing together a new group with no prior history, just do it! Take or make time to create the meeting specification in advance, and include the sharing and discussion of that specification as part of the flow of your first gathering.

Incorporating meeting specifications into existing groups—even those of which you're the leader—can be more difficult. Groups with established patterns of interaction may resist such changes, especially since the introduction of good meeting specifications and follow-up lists brings with it an additional layer of accountability for everyone involved. Be careful to introduce the new elements slowly, one or two at a time. Another good approach is to allocate time in one of your meetings to discuss a sample meeting specification you've created, so you can generate some discussion and agreement in the group about the value of adding a little more structure to the planning process.

If you're not the meeting's leader, you may feel an acute need for better meeting definition, but your chances of convincing the leader to make changes may be quite small. Remember, the information exchanged in the meeting may well include unspoken cues about levels of power and authority. Too strong a request for changes could represent an overt challenge to a covert structure; if your attempt is treated as such it will usually be met with either obvious or disguised hostility and resistance.

Stay true to your own purpose. Your goal as a culture builder is neither a hostile takeover nor an in-your-face introduction of major changes. It is the slow, steady adoption of manageable, incremental improvements by others who observe and mirror your role-modeling of overtness and clarity. If you can find a way to influence a change that's just large enough to have a positive impact, you may then have the opportunity to influence another one.

Even when you aren't able to influence someone else, you can always change your own behavior. A meeting may not have a formally published objective, but you can still make a tentative statement of your understanding of your group's purpose, then gently solicit members' feedback by asking them to help with your understanding. If you're asked to give a presentation without any indication of the expected outcome, you can still begin your talk by articulating your own version of the expected outcome—what you're planning to share and what you hope to accomplish—and soliciting feedback. Even in an accidental hallway gathering, you can pause to ask your colleagues about purpose if the conversation turns to a specific problem: "Do we want to try to reach a conclusion now, or shall we simply share information and plan to convene again later?"

Role-modeling is still your best approach.

Analyzing and Encouraging

We all know from experience just how frustrating ineffective group work can be. It's often somewhat less obvious when things are going well, especially when an improvement trend has just begun. As the culture builder, it's important that you become familiar with some positive indicators, so you can both recognize progress in the meetings you attend and role-model those positive behaviors to encourage others to replicate them.

Table 8.1 gives a scorecard you can use to analyze the groups with which you're involved. The first four positive aspects listed should come as no surprise, as we have already discussed them in detail: the existence of a lucid statement of the meeting's purpose, well-formed meeting specifications, effective follow-up lists, and appropriate membership lists. The remaining items depend on the type of interaction in which you're engaged. In information transfer, the primary focus is the overt and effective transfer of factual and hierarchical content, so the positive indicators are related to how well information is transferred. In a solution-oriented discussion, the central intent is to come to some conclusion, so the positive indicators are pertinent to the effectiveness of the group's problem-solving interactions.

The scorecard allows you to study your group work situations with an eye for what is working and what isn't. You allocate points based on positive indicators, with a higher score indicating a more effective meeting. This only provides a starting point; you can modify this template to suit your purposes. The important thing is to work within

Quick Video: Solve It Once

Visit www.MakeWorkGreat.com for a short video segment about how to solve a problem in a solution-oriented meeting. This is also an easy bit of information to share if you're trying to describe the contents of this chapter to a trusted friend or colleague.

TABLE 8.1 Checklist/Scorecard of Positive Indicators for Group Work of Both Types

All Purposes	Maximum Score
The meeting objective (purpose) is accurately defined and communicated in advance.	20 points
The meeting specification is written to include logistics and complete meeting flow and to focus time on most important issues only.	20 points
Follow-up lists and group memory are used effectively for action items, future agenda items, and later discussion items.	10 points
The meeting starts and ends on time according to the specification, or real-time adjustments are made in advance and overtly (as opposed to simply running over the scheduled time).	5 points

Information Transfer	Solution Generation	Maximum Score
A correctly defined membership list includes everyone who "needs to know."	A correctly defined membership list includes no more than 5–8 experts.	15 points
Information is given in brief, graphic presentations (maximum information transfer in minimum time).	A well-defined group problem-solving process focuses the group first on data accumulation, then on outcome or solution definition. (See sidebar on p. 189.)	10 points
Maximum overtness: hidden agendas are minimized in favor of aboveboard discussion of both factual and hierarchical information.	Balanced group interaction includes equal participation and contribution, eye contact (if in person), and requests for other members to share knowledge.	10 points
There is full communication of ratifications, decisions, and next steps by a defined and recognized chair or leader.	A predefined decision method clarifies in advance who will make the final decision and how it will be made. (See sidebar on p. 183.)	10 points
	TOTAL SCORE:	________/100

your sphere of influence, role-modeling good behavior patterns and encouraging more of what is already going well.

This scorecard is not, however, a comprehensive guide to human gatherings or a statistical analysis tool. It is but a small and preliminary glimpse into the very broad topic of group dynamics. The questions of how and why individuals behave differently when in groups—and of how those dynamics influence output, effectiveness, and stress—are complex ones. They provide the topics of many books already written and many more to come. Closely linked to issues of politics, power, and the importance of hierarchy, these issues fall well beyond the purview of our work here. For now, we simply wish to help you, the culture builder, demonstrate useful precedents to those around you.

As your influence expands, you may well decide that additional expertise in the area of group work would serve you well. If so, further study of group dynamics will be well worth your time. However far you take that study, the role-modeling of overtness and clarity will be your foundation.

The Invisible Assignment

If you're going to be leading, encouraging, or even just suggesting effective group work, you should know in advance that making groups great is a thankless job. If you do it poorly, if you're disruptive, or if for reasons beyond your control the group is a particularly difficult one, rest assured the "fault" for failure will most likely be assigned to you. Take care to constantly acknowledge the inherent complexity of group interactions, and be careful never to suggest that you have the guaranteed solution to the problem of meetings. Even the most talented, experienced group facilitators are quick to acknowledge that a situation can quickly get beyond their ability to help.

On the other hand, some of your meetings may go very well. If you help to build an environment in which everyone's expertise comes to the forefront at the right time and in the right way, and if you help your team to address the issues at hand smoothly and with minimal trouble, you will essentially be invisible. A select few may consciously recognize what you did, but the vast majority of participants will leave feeling good about what "they" accomplished and will have little understanding of the importance of your role. Some of them will say as much to you.

You must learn to absorb these inaccurate and frustrating comments silently and with humor. Actually, you should feel good about this outcome, because it is precisely in line with your culture-building goal: to present opportunities for others to benefit from and absorb your new patterns of behavior. All of the people who leave feeling good about what they accomplished may not associate that feeling with you, but they will associate it with the way in which they were working. This is positive reinforcement at its best; it is those patterns, not your personality, that they take with them. And when these satisfied people naturally attempt to repeat some of those patterns in other contexts of their own work lives, your cultural crystal grows.

Over time, as you become recognized as the common element across multiple engaged, productive group work scenarios, your influence will likely also increase in a more tangible way. Sooner or later, you'll find others approaching you for advice on how to successfully structure group work that falls into their area of responsibility.

When this happens, you can rest secure in the knowledge that you're getting better at finding the balance point between not enough change and too much change. You've found ways to make meaningful improvements in the output and pleasantness of the group work around you without activating fight-or-flight responses by asking for too much too quickly.

Regardless of your title, your background, or your previous experience, when you find yourself walking this balance beam successfully, you are practicing leadership within your cultural crystal. You have moved from advisor to definer.

EXERCISES

1. Make a list of the meetings you have attended over the past month and those you expect to attend over the next month. Which are primarily geared toward information transfer? Which are primarily geared toward problem solving? Which involve both purposes?

---

2. Choose the most useful or effective meeting you attended recently and score it using Table 8.1. Then choose the least useful or effective meeting in recent memory and score that one. What are the key differences between the productive meetings and time-wasters in your workplace?

---

3. Consider the meetings you plan to attend in the near future, and choose one over which you have some influence. How would you expect that meeting to score using Table 8.1? What can you do between now and the meeting—or during the meeting—to improve its effectiveness without inspiring resistance from other members by attempting to change too much?

---

4. Privately write a full meeting specification for a gathering you plan to attend, using Figure 8.3 as a guide, even though it may not be part of your role. Compare your results to the agenda or plan that will probably be used. How can you influence the existing agenda to align more closely with your meeting specification, yet not overstep your role?

---

9 You . . . as the Definer

In the popular 1990s cartoon series "Pinky and the Brain," two genetically enhanced talking lab mice made weekly comic and ill-fated bids for world domination. Ostensibly a children's program, the series had a good dose of adult humor as well, and it still has something of a cult following years later. Fans of many ages still recall the two-line dialogue that opened each and every episode:

PINKY: Gee, Brain, what do you want to do tonight?
BRAIN: The same thing we do every night, Pinky. Try to take over the world.

Hopefully, your own intentions in becoming a culture builder are not so absurdly megalomaniacal. (If they are, please review the comments about ethics in Chapter 1!) Yet our final chapter opens with this seemingly silly reference because it answers the question of what you should do once you've finally reached your highest level of cultural influence.

OTHER PERSON: Gee, now that you're a definer of culture, what do you want to do today?
YOU: The same thing I do every day. Try to be overt about tasks and seek clarity within relationships.

The Same Thing I Do Every Day

To some extent, most of us have participated in the "grass is greener over there" myth of leadership and management. We stand at our level of authority—whatever level that may be—and look with awe at the managers, leaders, and influencers above us on the organizational ladder or ahead of us in pay and responsibility. Whether or not we're striving to achieve those positions personally, we tend to suspect that those who are there have "arrived." Life there is somehow different, better, and easier than it is here.

When we do "arrive," reality rarely equals the fairy tale. Management and leadership at every level are difficult and fraught with potential land mines. Greater pay is nice, no doubt, but it typically comes with enough additional responsibility that familiar doubts about inadequate compensation quickly return. The learning curve that teaches us about the new position also strips away the awe and mystery, so in the final analysis, our escalated status is just another job—better in some ways, worse in others.

The same is true for your evolving role as a culture builder. When you first start to move from member to contributor, the role of definer seems distant, unattainable, and perhaps even a little magical. In reality, though, it's nothing of the sort. It is merely the next logical step in the progression. Keep practicing your disciplines of overtness and clarity, and you'll get there eventually. And, for better or worse, your "arrival" will be no arrival at all, just the gradual increase in your output and influence based on the repeated practice of your discipline. As your default patterns of behavior change, the change in precedent influences the patterns of those you work with. Viewed over time, as in Figure 9.1, the change is noticeable, both in you and in the people and patterns around you. But on a day-to-day basis, it won't seem like much at all. The only way to really appreciate the changes you've made will be to look back after six months or more on what is new with you and your environment.

In fact, much will be new. When the influence you exert has grown to this level, you'll be faced with new opportunities, new challenges, and many new questions. Issues of power, influence, group dynam-

FIGURE 9.1 The gradual change in your role influences precedent as it increases output

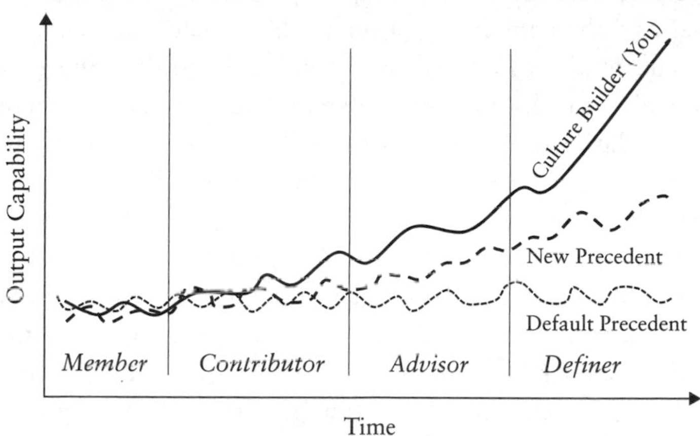

ics, hierarchy, and organizational structure will become a regular part of your life. The art and science of mobilizing progressively larger groups of people around an increasingly broadly defined common purpose likely will emerge as a lifelong challenge. Whether you address these questions through further study or real-life experience, you'll have an ever-growing need for their answers. As you can well imagine, this is a far broader course of study than this chapter—or even this book—can address.

Remember that no matter where you end up or how far you travel, your starting point never changes. No matter how large your cultural crystal becomes, the basic tenets of your seed crystal remain the same. What this final chapter will—and must—address is not the question of what you might end up doing differently as a definer of culture, but how to keep doing "the same thing you do every day."

Three Jobs You Must Not Take

Recall Emma, our role model of crystalline influence presented in Chapter 1. If you review her story now, you'll see immediately that she was operating as a definer by the time she and I met. She had a broad and stable cultural crystal of her own, which she used to create a platform to help me solve a complex problem. Despite her position of power and the complexity of the problems she was facing, Emma stayed true to the discipline of the culture builder. She practiced overtness about task to define problems and needs, and sought clarity within relationships to solicit support. She paid attention to both the tasks around her and the relationships required to make progress. She tended to her crystal, and her crystal supported her work.

Three things Emma did not do when suddenly faced with a new, complex, and serious problem that plagued her organization are tremendously instructive. First, she did not play the rescuer, staging a leadership takeover by claiming, "I'm the definer, and I'm in charge here." She neither promised nor attempted to save the day by taking command. Second, she did not play the persecutor, pointing at other people and other groups as "the real problem." She didn't use the power of her position to fire a cannon of blame at others who were lower in the hierarchy. Finally, she did not play the victim, claiming that she could do nothing until technical and organizational problems outside of her control were solved. She never spoke or acted in any way to suggest that she couldn't be instrumental in creating a solution.

Emma's three nonactions provide perfect examples of the three jobs you, as a culture definer, simply must not take: the rescuer, the persecutor, and the victim.

Obviously, these aren't jobs so much as they are roles. As we've been saying all along, from the perspective of culture building, your job title really isn't that important. It's not as though a director of sales, a level II customer service agent, an equipment engineer, a CPA, or anyone else can't practice overtness and clarity. Your title—any title—can't exclude you from defining new cultural precedents and demonstrating them to whomever is nearby.

What can exclude you—and will, instantly—is your choice to take on one of the three destructive roles mentioned above. Each will devastate your efforts at creating a new culture. Just as anyone at any level with any title can be a culture builder, anyone at any level with any title can take on the role of rescuer, victim, or persecutor and unwittingly bring their culture-changing efforts to a grinding halt.

Actually, there's a good chance you or someone you know has taken on one or more of these roles, accidentally or on purpose, in the last few days.

The Drama Triangle

In 1968, a psychologist named Stephen B. Karpman introduced a model for analyzing interpersonal relationships, which he labeled "the drama triangle." He identified three interrelated positions—the rescuer, the persecutor, and the victim—and explained that they comprise a transactional relationship, or a relationship that is characterized by a "game" between preestablished roles rather than by the actual interchange of factual and emotional information. In this game, each role prescribes how the player acts and reacts: the victim is saved by the rescuer from being taking advantage of by the persecutor. It's a basic pattern we all know well.[1]

Therein lies the problem. When we take on these roles, the challenge and reward of real information exchange is eliminated and replaced—first with the challenge and reward of scripted interaction, then with the challenge and reward of frequent role exchange. The roles play out, and then they switch. In the switch, the victim can become the persecutor, the rescuer can become the victim, and so on, so the game can continue, often at a higher level of intensity.

As a simple illustration of this game, consider one of Karpman's original examples, the children's fairy tale about Little Red Riding Hood. In this story, the dramatic interest is provided not by character development, but by the scripted interchange and surprise swapping between the three roles: Little Red Riding Hood begins as the rescuer of her grandmother and becomes the victim of the wolf; the wolf begins as Red's persecutor and becomes the victim of the woodsman. The story provides few real reasons for the players' actions, and that question somehow never comes up. Instead, the main characters play out their scripts until the plot lags, then the author switches their roles around to keep things interesting.[2]

You can probably replace this fairy tale with any number of stories from your own workplace. Perhaps a problem arises with a delivery schedule that's been promised to a customer. The project leader, playing rescuer to the customer, promises to save the day. He does so by forcing overtime commitments on the project team, thus becoming the persecutor of the team (his victims). Or an unscrupulous manager dishonestly shifts the blame for a software glitch to an uninvolved programmer who has made other mistakes in the past that cost other members of her group time and frustration. She plays persecutor to the programmer's victim because she wants to use the mistake as an excuse to fire the unpopular programmer, thereby playing rescuer to the rest of her team.

The possibilities are endless, and the scripts both compelling and commonplace. Yet this triumvirate—rescuer, persecutor, and victim—is the inventory of roles that you must avoid at all costs in your efforts to become a culture builder. The extent to which you fall short, taking on the predefined roles and acting out the associated scripts, is the extent to which you fail to demonstrate anything new to the people around you. When you're in a pre-scripted role, you're encouraging others to take on related roles and discouraging them from spending their energy on the exchange of real information.

In the crystalline network, you can be a contributor of intelligence or a blind follower of preordained roles, but you can't be both.

Don't Be a Rescuer

If you follow the advice in this book, you're likely to get some positive results, possibly in fairly short order. When you do, and others begin to look to you for guidance, some of them will unwittingly cast you in the role of rescuer: "Kate saved us. Kate figured it out when nobody else could. Kate did the work of two people in half the time. Kate is an asset to all of us." It would seem on the surface that it's very good to be Kate.

To be a rescuer, however, is to be set up for a fall. As you complete this book, you should have some good ideas about how to bring more functionality to your workplace. You may also have some notions about how to better manage your peers and employees. But, as you well know, you still don't have all the answers to life. If anything, the tools offered here have equipped you to uncover even more unanswerable questions than you faced before and, at best, to feel somewhat comfortable with the resulting ambiguity. You're not imbued with magical powers to make everything better, and you certainly won't be able to solve every problem or slay every dragon set before you.

Should anyone mistakenly begin to regard you as if you had such magical abilities, it's in your best interest to put a stop to it quickly. Such treatment quickly leads to jealousy on the part of former rescuers, who perceive themselves as having been dethroned, and to unrealistic expectations on the part of your worshippers. Either of those misperceptions has the potential to sabotage you and destroy your credibility, your effectiveness, and your ability to increase the reach of your new cultural patterns.

Instead, be quick to share credit and recognize the culturally beneficial contributions of others. Be gracious but firm: "I appreciate the encouragement, but as I say at every opportunity, I was only a piece of a larger puzzle, a cog in a much larger machine. Jane did such a good job defining the goal in terms of the customers' needs, and Terry was so effective at giving us visibility about our progress, that my part of the solution happened automatically." Courteously accept compliments, but don't allow them to define you.

Don't Be a Persecutor

As you achieve a modicum of success with your culture-building efforts, you will also begin to regard your new patterns of behavior as giving some good answers to the question of how people should behave at work. Add some pressure to produce output and a bit of responsibility over projects, peers, or staff members, and you have the recipe for a persecutor in the making.

"After all," you may argue, "it's my function as manager (team leader, advisor, and so on) to advise others, set expectations, and encourage and reward performance relative to those expectations." True enough, but you must be very specific with yourself about what happens when you set an expectation—such as instructing everyone to craft a summary outputs list—and someone fails to fulfill it. What is your response to the person who laughs off your novel and adamant insistence on the adoption of new cultural patterns? What about the person who calls it "just another program du jour" or "the latest in the string of useless books you're reading"? You may well be tempted to set that person straight, to put him in his place. You may sense that it's time to "show everyone who's boss." If someone pushes just the right button, you'll face that temptation head-on.

Depending on your status and role in the organization, you may also be well positioned for the challenge. Maybe you have direct authority over the troublesome person in question and can make all the right negative words show up on his next formal performance review. Or perhaps you have a good relationship with someone much higher in the organization and can, with a well-placed comment, encourage all the weight of that position to come cascading down on the thorn in your side. You'll make him see the error of his ways, and in the process, you'll show everyone else that you're not to be trifled with. The problem in taking this approach is that you'll also become the persecutor whom nobody trusts and with whom no one wants to share information. All the work you've put into role-modeling new patterns will go out the window, along with your reputation for fairness and equanimity.

Don't be afraid to redirect a challenge to your new patterns rather than engage. If you have true confidence in what you're doing, continued role-modeling will either bring your problematic colleague around or make his objections irrelevant as he is wrapped in the new patterns by everyone else in your crystalline network. Verbalize and acknowledge your differences of opinion, and use your patterns of overtness and clarity in your discussions about expectations. Whatever you do, never cease to be respectful of the other person: "Obviously, you and

I don't see this the same way. I need your help in finding some middle ground. I want you to have the chance to test this out on your own, but obviously we can't have you simply ignoring the expectations set for you and your peers. Please help me here." Don't just say it; mean it.

Don't Be a Victim

If you're in the business of building new cultures, you're going to get plenty of invitations to be a victim.

You've already passed on the first such opportunity. You could have chosen to be a victim of "the way things have always been done." Having gotten through this book, you deserve kudos for making a different choice. But rest assured there will be others suggesting that you play a victim role: the highly influential manager who feels threatened by your new level of output; the difficult employee who refuses to adopt the new patterns you request; and the heavyweight customer who insists on vaguely defined, ever-changing output from you. Each of these people is going to tempt you to become a victim again and again. They will encourage you to sit down, shut up, and stop trying.

It's all too big to really change it. Why bother making the effort?

Take care to choose your mental frameworks for your actions based on reality, not on prewritten scripts. If you've been experimenting with an approach that doesn't seem to be working, if your priorities have changed, or if a new environment mandates that you take different action, a change in your strategy may be the intelligent move. If your decision is a rational one, if you've learned from your experiment and decided to make a change, then this is not being a victim because you're not playing "loser" to another person's "winner." On the other hand, if what you're attempting continues to make sense in the context of your goals and ethics and the requirements of the broader situation, then the abandonment of those efforts because you "just can't win" is scarcely in anyone's best interest. Framing yourself as the victim of a person or precedent that is more assertive, louder, or more threatening than you demoralizes those around you. Perhaps more importantly, it fails to showcase the inherent intelligent function of the new cultural patterns you've been trying to demonstrate. Adopting the victim role reflects poorly on the utility of the behaviors you've been attempting to display, and the loss of your credibility takes with it some of the impact of many weeks, months, or years of role-modeling.

It's not necessary that you lose or that someone else wins. The definitions of success are far more flexible, and they are constantly made and adjusted by both parties. Don't get entrenched! You can reframe an incoming "attack"—perhaps, for example, a seemingly aggressive complaint from an outspoken customer—as an expression of information. You can respond to that information without framing it as a win-or-lose scenario: "One of our goals is to support our top-tier customers with 100 percent response to issues and improvement requests," you might tell your team. "We're learning, however, that one such customer is particularly rapid and variable in the pace and content of those requests, probably because of its particular business constraints. How can we refine our purpose or reallocate our resources to maximize our ability to meet that customer's needs, while still keeping it in balance with our other work?" Such a conversation held internally may be a good first step; including the difficult customer in a similar conversation might be the second.

Avoid the Three Roles at All Costs

Once you become aware of the three undesirable roles, you'll begin to see them everywhere in the workplace. Table 9.1 lists some of their more common manifestations. When directed at you, these manifestations strongly encourage you to fall back into pre-scripted roles. Learning to recognize them and treat them as red-flag warnings to monitor your own response is well worth your time.

Of course, your best response is heavily situation dependent, and the examples of exit tactics offered in this chapter are necessarily somewhat simplistic. They won't work in every situation, and they may not work for you. But they do illustrate ways of disallowing the activation of role-based scripts by turning the conversational

TABLE 9.1 Common Workplace Manifestations of the Three Roles to Avoid

Rescuer	Persecutor	Victim
Cheerleading	Blaming	Just following orders
Fighting "the power" or planning a coup	Criticizing	Deflecting blame
Helping or tending to "the wounded"	Shaming	Being cynical
Playing Mr./Ms. Fix-It	Covertly "sniping" or backstabbing	Displaying hopelessness

focus back to the exchange of real, useful, complex information or distinctions.

When one tactic to help you exit the role of rescuer, persecutor, or victim fails, don't hesitate to try another—and another and another and another, until you find a way out of whichever role has entrapped you. Remember that the roles are not real. Speak out loud to yourself, or write in your notebook, "I will not play this pre-scripted role!" As a definer of culture, you must also be an experimenter, learning from the results of your own actions and using what you learn to inform your future attempts. Be vigilant in noticing, avoiding, and exiting from the three roles of the drama triangle.

Why? Because these roles are to the crystalline network what a virus is to a computer network. They start at one node and quickly spread negative action patterns to neighboring nodes. The pre-scripted, time-wasting, and useless patterns take over each node, one at a time, and replace productive processing power with the ineffective burning of energy and calories. Just like a computer virus, if left unchecked, the drama triangle virus ultimately bogs down the whole system and brings productive output to a halt. Don't let it happen to your crystal. As the definer, you must be the one who defines the situation differently.

You Are the Starting Point

How can you possibly avoid the propagation of this "virus"? As we have discussed many times in this book, it's all about what *you* do. Long before you became a definer, you made the conscious choice to become the point of origination of new patterns of behavior for those close to you in the crystalline network. This was your prologue, the "decision to decide" that you made before you started. As your influence increased, your continued, disciplined practice of overtness and clarity naturally kept leading you to the proper decisions and actions. By the time you reach the level of definer, those practices will be working, and those decisions and actions will be coming from you habitually.

Through those same practices, you can avoid the three detrimental roles of rescuer, persecutor, and victim. You will practice overtness about task, defining goals in terms of what they are (purpose), what their accomplishment implies to the organization (impact), how advances toward them are made visible (progress), what they require (resources), and how they affect the individuals working on them (incentive and capability). You will also practice clarity within relationships, carefully defining the questions behind any interaction,

Quick Video: Stop the Drama and Do the Work

Visit www.MakeWorkGreat.com for a short video segment about how to recognize and avoid the three roles of the drama triangle. This is also an easy bit of information to share if you're trying to describe the contents of this chapter to a trusted friend or colleague.

being cautious to employ the most useful and respectful approach to others, and defining the need for agreement as narrowly as possible in each situation. You need only make your discipline strong enough to guide you in every situation, and you will automatically avoid the drama triangle; its three pre-scripted roles simply cannot exist at the same time as real overtness and clarity. The roles are not real.

Stay true to your patterns and your continued success as definer will take care of itself. Your discipline will naturally lead you to make adjustment as needed by paying attention to the cues around you and modifying your own behavior so that you continue to influence your environment without engendering resistance. This is not to say that you will make perfect decisions, take perfect actions, or never fall into the trap of playing one of the three roles. But the stronger and more consistent your discipline, the more likely you will make fewer such mistakes and recognize and correct the ones you do make more quickly. Your decisions will tend to optimize the ratio of output versus stress. And in the inevitable moments when an improved culture or a more enjoyable workplace experience seem impossibly out of reach, your exit from hopelessness will be far quicker if you diligently maintain your patterns.

Evaluating Advice

Take equal care to employ your practices of overtness and clarity and to avoid the roles of the drama triangle when evaluating suggestions from others. As we've said and you've surely realized, you will face many situations beyond what can be addressed in this book; the complex issues already mentioned—group dynamics, power, and hierarchy—are just a few examples. Seemingly credible advice regarding these topics abounds, and as you become a definer of culture and your influence grows, such advice will come at you from all angles. Those ahead of you and higher up in your organization will offer it, framed as helpful suggestions, admonitions, or perhaps thinly veiled words of warning. Peers and employees will offer it, perhaps as formal 360-degree feedback or as informal sharing of what they've seen others in your position do successfully. And external experts will offer it—footnoted with an impressive variety of degrees, credentials, and references—via books, webcasts, seminars, and consultations, free or for a fee. The spirit in which the advice is offered and the agendas of those offering it will differ widely and may not always be easy to deduce.

The quality of the advice itself, however, can be evaluated far more simply. Whoever you think you can believe, whatever advice you consider following, check it first with two straightforward tests:

1. Is it consistent with your disciplines of overtness and clarity?

2. Does it support your avoidance of the roles of rescuer, persecutor, and victim?

If it passes both tests, then it may be worth considering. But if it fails either one—if it runs counter to your practice of overtness and clarity, or if it encourages you toward or traps you in the three scripts of the drama triangle—walk away from it quickly! No matter where it comes from, no matter how impressive the credentials or noble the intentions of the person offering it, such advice does not benefit you. As compelling as it may be, it will ultimately serve only to disrupt the very crystal you've tried so hard to build.

Nothing Left but the Doing

With that, it seems we've run out of things to talk about. Thank goodness! We have covered a lot of ground in a relatively small number of pages. We began with just a mind-set, the choice to change. We moved quickly to workplace practices for you to use alone and ultimately ended up suggesting ways to mobilize groups of people and to role-model patterns of activity for an increasingly large environment.

Some might argue that we've covered enough material for more than one book. Yet all we've really done is explore the various manifestations and ramifications of two simple principles: overtness about task and clarity within relationship. First, be overt about the work you're doing—your purpose, the impact your work will create, your personal incentives, visibility into your progress, the resources you need, and the capability you have to achieve it. Second, seek clarity in the relationships you have with others—clarity of the question you need to address, the approach you'll use, and the need for agreement between you.

Everything else we've talked about, everything else you've thought about as you read, and everything else you'll do as a culture builder is nothing more or less than implementation, the act of taking the best next logical step to continue to optimize your output-stress ratio.

Of course, *logical* doesn't necessarily mean "easy." If it did, if this were as easy to do as it is to understand, everyone would be doing it already. Obviously, everyone is not doing it. You are. In that difference—in the intentional, conscious, self-directed choice you've made to do something other than what everyone else is doing—lies the hidden energy you harness to change your workplace and your world. With skill and a little luck, you'll use that energy wisely, and it will serve you well.

You're in Better Shape than You May Think

The crystalline network of the early information age workplace is complicated, thorny, multidimensional, and messy. But it is also, in its own way, an elegant, pragmatic structure.

Remember the old expression that "a chain is only as strong as its weakest link"? That expression applies to chains, not to networks. The whole idea of networks—the reason they're employed by the complex systems that support our e-mail and Internet searches, for example—is that they're far less susceptible to poor performance by a single node. When one link in a chain breaks, the chain is broken. But when one node in a network stops functioning, the network adapts. E-mail has many paths it can travel between your desk and mine. When the shortest or quickest path is not available, another one is selected.

This is not to say that we should idly permit faulty nodes to thrive in our networks. Both our computer networks and our crystalline workplace structures benefit when we raise the quality of all nodes involved. Performance upgrades are good for the system.

But they don't have to happen all at once. We don't go out and upgrade the whole Internet. At any given time, some nodes perform better than others. Sometimes we fix or remove the less-functional units; other times we enhance the output of the high performers. Either strategy is good for overall performance. And sometimes, when things are working well enough, we just sit back and let the network do its thing.

When you avoid the viral roles of rescuer, persecutor, and victim, and instead focus on real information transfer (on practicing overtness about your tasks and clarity within your relationships), you become a high-performing node. In following the guidance of this book, you also begin to influence many of the nodes around you—your neighbors in both the physical and the metaphorical sense—to be high performers too.

At the end of the day, that's all you or anyone else can do. After all, an organization is nothing more than the people who comprise it. All output of the computer network comes from one or more of the computers within it, and all output of the human organization comes from one or more of the humans within it. You are no more or less a part of that network than anyone else, no more or less a part of it than you choose to be. If there's a problem with the way your business world works, it lies in that network. Any solution—any strategy to make work great—lies there as well. It must, because there is nothing else—nothing to complain about, nothing to influence, nothing to benefit from, and nothing to enjoy—other than yourself and the people around you.

This book opened with a note of warning. You're not as autonomous as you think you are. Be aware of the choices you make.

It closes now with a note of hope and gratitude for the benefit we all receive from the crystalline network. To make a real change, interdependence—not autonomy—is the key. You can encourage the people who were pulling *on* you to pull *with* you instead. Given the complexity of the world we live in, we can all thank goodness for that.

EXERCISES

1. Write a two-paragraph snapshot of your environment when you first began your culture-changing attempts. List what was going well and your areas of greatest concern. After 6 to 12 months, revisit that description and see what has changed. Revisit it again every 6 to 12 months, each time writing a new synopsis of the current environment. If you're making an impact, it will be far more visible in this exercise than on a day-to-day basis.

2. When was the last time you saw others in your workplace playing out the three roles of rescuer, persecutor, and victim? Make note of a situation you observed in which two or more people were adopting and exchanging those roles, following scripts rather than taking self-directed, effective actions. What would have helped their situation?

3. When was the last time you yourself engaged in one or more of these three roles? What set of circumstances encouraged you into the role(s)? How might you have handled the situation differently if you hadn't had the scripted role requirements? What did you do—or what can you do—to help yourself remember that the roles are not real and engineer an escape from them?

4. What advice have you received recently that seemed sound? Was it in keeping with your disciplines of overtness and clarity? Will it help you avoid the three viral roles of the drama triangle? If not, can you adjust the implementation of the advice so it will be consistent with your new behavior patterns?

5. This is the last question in the book and may also be the most important. What is the first thing that you are going to start doing differently and consistently as a result of what you've read? How will y-o-u begin to practice overtness about task and clarity within relationships, to begin to change your own crystalline network? In other words, how do you intend to make your workplace great?

Appendix: Summary of Video Lessons

All videos can be viewed at www.MakeWorkGreat.com.

Chapter 1

"Burn Your Org Chart"—how the onset of the information age has changed the structure of the workplace

Chapter 2

"Say No Without Saying No"—how to construct and use a "verbalized summary outputs (or objectives)" list as a statement of your workplace purpose

"Six Hidden Factors of Motivation"—six factors that often incentivize us at work

Chapter 3

"Smart Managers Read Behavior"—how to define the pace and content of your approach to another person (whether or not you are a manager)

Chapter 4

"Encouraging Excellent Performance"—how to encourage someone to replicate a positive behavior

"Changing Behavior"—how to advise someone regarding a gap in skills or performance

Chapter 5

"Manage the People Managing You"—how to use the ICE model (identify, connect, explain) with your role set

Chapter 6

"Disagree, Don't Argue"—how to use the five building blocks of reality to improve your communications

Chapter 7

"Improving Output"—how to advise others using the six forms of overtness about task

Chapter 8

"Meeting Types—Information vs. Solution"—how to recognize and utilize the two types of meetings
"Turbocharge Your Meetings"—how to add expected outcomes to your meeting plans
"Group Decision Making That Works"—how to define the process for agreement in a group setting
"Solve It Once"—how to solve a problem in a solution-oriented meeting

Chapter 9

"Stop the Drama and Do the Work"—how to recognize and avoid the three roles of the drama triangle

Notes

Prologue

1. James B. Maas and Kathleen M. Toivanen, "Candid Camera and the Behavioral Sciences," *Teaching of Psychology* 5 no. 4 (1978): 226–28, informaworld.com/10.1207/s15328023top0504_17.
2. Solomon E. Asch, "Opinions and Social Pressure," *Scientific American* 193 (1955): 31–35, wadsworth.com/psychology_d/templates/student_resources/0155060678_rathus/ps/ps18.html.
3. Sandra Blakeslee, "What Other People Say May Change What You See," *New York Times*, June 28, 2005, zainea.com/social conformity.htm.
4. Stanley Milgram, "Obedience to Authority," 1974, PanArchy, panarchy.org/milgram/obedience.html.
5. Philip Zimbardo, "The Power of Norms and Groups on Individuals: Parallels Between the Stanford Prison Experiment and Milgram's Obedience Research," *The Lucifer Effect* (deleted content not included in book), lucifereffect.org/about_content_norms.htm.
6. William R. Daniels, *Breakthrough Performance Managing for Speed and Flexibility* (Mill Valley, CA: ACT Publishing, 1995), 10–15.

7. Daniel Katz and Robert L. Kahn, *The Social Psychology of Organizations* (New York: John Wiley & Sons, 1966), 185–190.
8. James Surowiecki, "The Fatal-Flaw Myth," *The New Yorker*, July 31, 2006, newyorker.com/archive/2006/07/31/060731ta_talk_surowiecki.
9. Susan M. Andersen and Philip G. Zimbardo, "Resisting Mind Control," *U.S.A. Today* (an educational journal) 109 (1980): 44–47.
10. Jay Shafritz and J. Steven Ott, eds., *Classics of Organization Theory* (Fort Worth, TX: Harcourt College Publishers, 2001), 373–4; quoted in Symphony Orchestra Institute, *Organizational Culture*, soi.org/reading/change/culture.shtml.
11. Solomon E. Asch, "Opinions and Social Pressure," *Scientific American* 193 (1955): 31–35, wadsworth.com/psychology_d/templates/student_resources/0155060678_rathus/ps/ps18.html.

Chapter 1

1. Edward Muzio, Deborah Fisher, and Erv Thomas, *Four Secrets to Liking Your Work: You May Not Need to Quit to Get the Job You Want* (Upper Saddle River, NJ: FT Press, 2008), 1–2.
2. John Lazar and Brenda Smith, "The Business Case for Coaching in Organizations" (presented at International Society for Performance Improvement Fall Conference, Albuquerque, NM, September 2008).
3. Carol Spiers, "Smaller Business Equals Less Stress," Gulfnews.com Business Opinion, December 15, 2009, http://gulfnews.com/business/opinion/smaller-business-equals-less-stress-1.553553.
4. Lazar & Smith 2008.
5. Kristina Cowan, "Can Job Hopping Hurt Your Career?" AOL Find a Job/Career Builder, August 10, 2009, http://jobs.aol.com/article/_a/can-job-hopping-hurt-your-career/20080227121109990001?ncid=AOLCOMMjobsDYNLprim0001.
6. Muzio et al., *Four Secrets to Liking Your Work*, 1–2.

7. Thumbay Group–UAE, "Two-Thirds of Employees Want to Quit Work," daijiworld.com, February 12, 2008, daijiworld.com/news/news_disp.asp?n_id=43425&n_tit=UAE%3A+Two-thirds+of+Employees+Want+to+Quit+Work.
8. "40% of Employees Want to Quit Job—Survey," BreakingNews.ie, August 10, 2004, breakingnews.ie/archives/?c=BUSINESS&jp=kfqlauauqlql&d=2004-10-08.
9. Sarah Cook, Steve Macaulay, and Hilary Coldicott, *Change Management Excellence: Using the Four Intelligences for Successful Organizational Change* (Sterling, VA: Kogan Page, 2004), 60.
10. William E. Schneider, *The Reengineering Alternative: A Plan for Making Your Current Culture Work* (Burr Ridge, IL: Irwin Professional, 1994), 142.
11. Daniel Goleman, *Social Intelligence: The New Science of Human Relationships* (New York: Bantam Books, 2006), 15–16.
12. John P. Kotter. *Leading Change* (Boston: Harvard Business School Press, 1996), 25–30.
13. Richard S. Guha, *How to Get What You Want Most in Life: Achieve Worldly and Emotional Career Success* (Bloomington, IN: iUniverse, 2004), 67.
14. Robert Maurer, *One Small Step Can Change Your Life: The Kaizen Way* (New York: Workman Publishing, 2004).

Chapter 2

1. William R. Daniels, *Breakthrough Performance*, 28–29.
2. Geary A. Rummler and Alan P. Brache, *Improving Performance: How to Manage the White Space on the Organization Chart* (San Francisco: Jossey-Bass, 1995), 434.
3. Clark L. Wilson, *How and Why Effective Managers Balance Their Skills* (Boulder, CO: Clark Wilson Group, 2003), 17.
4. Ken Blanchard and Sheldon Bowles, *Gung Ho!* (New York: William Morrow, 1997), 169.

5. Edward Muzio, Deborah Fisher, and Erv Thomas, *Four Secrets to Liking Your Work: You May Not Need to Quit to Get the Job You Want* (Upper Saddle River, NJ: FT Press, 2008), 45–73.

Chapter 3

1. Muzio et al., *Four Secrets*, 22–23.
2. See the video about Sun CEO Jonathan Schwartz, which opens with the company's vision statement: sun.com/aboutsun/executives/schwartz/bio.jsp.
3. Ola Svenson and A. John Maule, "Time pressure and stress in human judgment and decision making," *Springer* (1993): 36–37.
4. Gary A. Klein, *How People Make Decisions*, 2nd ed. (Cambridge, MA: MIT Press, 1999), 275–6.
5. Joshua Rubinstein and David Meyer, "Is Multitasking More Efficient? Shifting Mental Gears Costs Time, Especially When Shifting to Less Familiar Tasks," August 5, 2001, from http://www.apa.org/releases/multitasking.html, citing Rubenstein, Meyer, and Evans, "Executive Control of Cognitive Processes in Task Switching," *Journal of Experimental Psychology, Human Perception and Performance*, 27, no. 4: 763–97.
6. Gerald A. Cory and Russell Gardner, *The Evolutionary Neuroethology of Paul MacLean: Convergences and Frontiers* (Santa Barbara, CA: Greenwood Publishing Group, 2002), 57.

Chapter 4

1. Daniels, *Breakthrough Performance*, 239.
2. Ibid., 231.

Chapter 5

1. Edward Muzio, "Manage the People Managing You," BNET/CBS Interactive Video, http://www.bnet.com/2422-13731_23-265802.html.

Chapter 6

1. David T. Neal, Wendy Wood, and Jeffrey M. Quinn, "Habits—a Repeat Performance," *Current Directions in Psychological Science* 15, no. 4 (2006): 198.
2. Henry H. Yin and Barbara J. Knowlton, "The Role of the Basal Ganglia in Habit Formation," *Nature Reviews Neuroscience* 7 (June 2006): 464–76, http://e.guigon.free.fr/rsc/article/YinKnowlton06.pdf.
3. Stephanie A. Burns, "Installing a New Habit and Breaking an Old One," Stephanie Burns Articles, stephanieburns.com/articles/article06_habit.asp.
4. Scott H. Young, "18 Tricks to Make New Habits Stick," Stepcase Lifehack, August 4, 2007, lifehack.org/articles/productivity/18-tricks-to-make-new-habits-stick.html.
5. Yin and Knowlton, "The Role of the Basal Ganglia."
6. Karen Pryor, *Don't Shoot the Dog! The New Art of Teaching and Training* (New York: Bantam Books, 1999), 2.
7. Daniel Katz, "Nationalism and Strategies of International Conflict Resolution," in *International Behavior: A Social Psychological Analysis*, ed. H. C. Kelman (New York: Holt, Rinehart & Winston, 1965), 356–90.
8. Ron Fisher, "Sources of Conflict and Methods of Conflict Resolution," International Peace and Conflict Resolution, School of International Service, The American University, 2000, aupeace.org/files/Fisher_SourcesofConflictandMethodsofResolution.pdf (accessed February 12, 2009).
9. Daniel Katz and Robert L. Kahn, *The Social Psychology of Organizations* (New York: John Wiley & Sons, 1966), 177–79, 184–85.
10. Roger Fisher and William Ury, *Getting to Yes: Negotiating Agreement Without Giving In*, ed. Bruce Patton (New York: Penguin Books, 1991), 17–55.

Chapter 8

1. Gayle W. Hill, "Group Versus Individual Performance: Are N+1 Heads Better Than One?" *Psychological Bulletin* 91, no. 3 (1982): 517–39.
2. Andrew S. Grove, *High Output Management* (New York: Random House, 1985), 72–87.
3. William R. Daniels, *Group Power II: A Manager's Guide to Conducting Regular Meetings* (Mill Valley, CA: University Associates Inc., 1990), 4–5.

Chapter 9

1. Stephen B. Karpman, "Fairy Tales and Script Drama Analysis," *Transactional Analysis Bulletin* 7, no. 26 (1968): 39–43, karpmandramatriangle.com/pdf/DramaTriangle.pdf.
2. Karpman, "Fairy Tales."

Index